Output Measures
for School Library
Media Programs

Frances Bryant Bradburn

Neal-Schuman Publishers, Inc.
New York   London

Published by Neal-Schuman Publishers, Inc.
100 Varick Street
New York, NY 10013-1506

Printed and bound in the United States of America

Library of Congress Cataloging-in-Publication Data
Bradburn, Frances Bryant.
    Output measures for school media programs / Frances Bryant Bradburn.
        p.   cm.
    Includes bibliographical references and index.
    ISBN 1-55570-326-7 (alk. paper)
    1. School libraries--Evaluation--Statistical methods.
  2. Instructional materials centers--Evaluation--Statistical methods.
  I. Title.
  Z675.S3B685   1999   98-45557
  027.8--dc21   CIP

To my mother who nurtured the potential
    Gerald who helped me recognize the potential
    My children who kept life "sweet" even during the hard times
    And John ... of course.

Contents

List of Figures

List of Data Collection Forms

Foreword

Evaluating your school library media program is essential if you are to attract and maintain the support you need to provide the range of resources and services required to meet the information, curricular, and recreational needs of your students and faculty. In the past, most evaluation and documentation efforts focused on circulation statistics, title and volume counts, attendance figures, and librarian/teacher interactions. While these counts may have provided interesting data, they did little to enable school library media professionals to make compelling arguments when funding for programs was threatened. In this age of accountability, it is no longer enough to say that good libraries are important for good schools. It is critical that we as library media professionals have the research and the data to demonstrate how quality library programs contribute to student learning and effective teaching.

Output Measures for School Library Media Programs, based upon the highly successful and widely used tools developed in the public library field, can be used to justify budget allocations, encourage flexible scheduling, support requests for staffing increases, or promote program expansions. The measure can be used singly or in combination depending upon the need. The directions for collecting and analyzing the data are clear and potential problems are clearly identified. Whether you are a newcomer to the school library media field or a veteran in the profession, this book can help you make the arguments needed to ensure continued support for your program.

The mission of the school library media program is to ensure that students and staff are effective users of ideas and information. However, this mission cannot be accomplished unless the program has strong administrative support and adequate resources to ensure that the needed support and resources for library media programs continue in times of revolving administrative leadership, shrinking budgets, and competing priorities. Systematic, logical arguments must be developed. I urge you to use the tools provided in *Output Measures for School Library Media Programs* on an ongoing basis to build and strengthen your current program and to protect it in times of potential cutbacks. This ongoing documentation and evaluation will undoubtedly result in library media programs that will more effectively meet the information needs of our students and faculty— and isn't that what our profession is all about!

Ann Carlson Weeks, Ph.D.
Director of Libraries and Information Services
Chicago Public Schools

Preface

School library media programs do improve teaching and learning. From Lance to Loertscher to Library Power, research shows that quality resources and library services make a difference in student self-esteem, school climate, and ultimately even test scores. Even *The Places Rated Almanac* has recognized the importance of school library media centers to the overall quality of a school system.

Yet in order to provide the library media collections and services needed to make a difference in a child's education, schools must allocate a great deal of money for salaries, collections, and facilities beyond the classroom. Regardless of the research, in this day of limited resources and instant results, school library media specialists too often find themselves fighting for even an adequate portion of any school budget.

At best, this struggle for fiscal resources is nonproductive; at worst, it is divisive. Yet how can we move beyond it to focus on what is best for a child's education and development, for a teacher's ability to teach, for the nurturing of lifelong learning in general? By using statistics. Yes, statistics! Logical, well-conceived arguments based on data from our own, unique, school library media centers will often convince even the most fiscally shell-shocked administrator — and a roomful of classroom teachers. Numbers are concrete proof that a problem exists — and that something is being done to support classroom teachers. Thus the goals of *Output Measures for School Library Media Programs* are:

- to give school library media specialists a variety of output measures that allow them ample proof of what works and does not work within their media program.

- to make sure that school library media specialists have procedures that can document and analyze not only resources — books, equipment, software — but the library media program as well: the curriculum support fill rate and the media center use rate, for example.

- to give school library media specialists the tools to make a case for resources, staff, or schedule.

Using statistics to justify our programs is not a new strategy. We have all, at one time or another, calculated the average copyright date of our collections or tracked circulation statistics. We also have taken stock of our collections to see if they will support the new environmental education unit the science teacher is proposing, or the new health education standards mandated by the state. But many of us have kept this information to ourselves. Lacking a specific format and process for calculation and reporting, we have logged this invaluable information in our heads or somewhere in our collection development file, planned our next few orders, and gone on with our work.

How much more effective might our library media programs be if we began a process to make individuals throughout our school community aware of exactly what is going on within our media centers — what resources are currently available to students and teachers, what is happening now within the media center, and what *could* happen with a few more targeted resources, a few more volunteers, or even a half-time assistant! *Output Measures for School Library Media Programs* can help you create a format for taking information already available or traditionally collected by school library media specialists, use it to talk about existing programs, and offer documentation for programs change.

How This Book Evolved

Since 1985 I have had one of the most satisfying jobs imaginable — working with North Carolina's school library media specialists. In this capacity I have helped many of them organize a process to provide information to teachers, parents, administrators, and even school boards that justifies additional funding for collections, equipment and staffing. Over the years, I realized that the more concrete our arguments were, the more successful an individual media specialist or system-level supervisor would be in presenting his or her case for funding or schedule changes. Decision-makers appreciated a carefully documented, well-reasoned justification for additional resources. It appeared that they believed a direct correlation existed between documentation and stewardship. It also gave them an acceptable, logical justification for awarding what, at least in their minds, was a large amount of money.

Simultaneously, I observed with interest the publication of a series of books about output measures — for public libraries, academic libraries, children's services and, later, YA services. Frankly I was skeptical. It just seemed like too much paperwork! When, in a typical school library media specialist's day, would anyone find the time to do all this? Gradually, however, I realized that we all were tiptoeing around the inevitable. Loertscher and Ho were teaching us how to map collections, Marilyn Miller and Marilyn Shontz were tracking funding yearly in *School Library Journal*, and Shontz was even tying output measures to job performance. It was time to analyze and carefully organize a process that was successful in justifying programmatic change, thanks to trial and error and the good thinking of myriad school librarians and academicians. I decided that I was ready — and eager — to undertake the analysis and organization so that other school library media specialists could skip the trial and error stage. With this goal in mind, I wrote *Output Measures for School Library Media Programs*.

Who Should Use This Book?

The easy answer to this question is that all school library media specialists should use this book, because documenting media center use will eventually benefit everyone. But let's examine the bigger picture.

Funding, staffing, and scheduling problems are seldom isolated within one school in a district. Although some school library media specialists may serve more affluent sections of a system, budget woes tend to affect a whole district. Therefore, a systemwide focus by all school library media specialists on one particular need — additional funding for all schools, a media assistant in all centers — can be a highly effective use of everyone's time. Together, all district media personnel determine the measures to be collected, the sampling dates, and the format for reporting. A designated person or persons can merge the information into a systemwide report. The group then can authorize an individual or individuals to present the report to the appropriate person.

Obviously, a systemwide focus such as this requires an extraordinary level of oversight of the process and organization of the data into one massive report. Everyone needs to buy into the process, and those individuals who agree to merge and report the information are taking on a formidable job. A systemwide commitment stands the best chance of success if a media supervisor is in place to spearhead the process, helping those school library media specialists who need it and compiling the data for the districtwide report. But what if your system does not employ a media supervisor or you cannot get buy-in from everyone? Can you do this alone? Definitely! It may be even more effective if you target your own principal or PTA for your school's particular needs. In this case, you target the areas of your collection or the staffing or scheduling issue you wish to address, choose the measures most appropriate for your position, and begin the process.

How This Book Is Organized

As you flip through the pages of *Output Measures for School Library Media Programs*, you will notice that it is divided into two distinct sections. The first section defines and explains the measures themselves; the second section contains three case studies that simulate the data-gathering and presentation process.

A section is devoted to each measure, defining it and explaining the data collection methods. Sample tracking forms and work sheets, which you can photocopy or reconstruct, are often included so that you don't have to "re-invent the wheel." Of course, you may have a better way to design your forms. That's fine. The important thing here is the process of data gathering, not the form itself.

Finally, you will be walked through the process of how to analyze and use the data. Occasionally you'll find Hot Spots! that alert you to the possible pitfalls of documenting or analyzing a particular measure. Sometimes these Hot Spots! relate directly to what might happen when you present the data. Other times they offer thoughts about what the data may actually reveal about your program or collection.

At the end of each section there is a Measure at a Glance box, which summarizes the use of the measure, shows how to calculate it and, when appropriate, refers you to the case study that illustrates its use. When you actually do your calculations, you can refer to the Quick Reference for All Output Measures, which is found on the inside covers. This is handy when all you need is to see the formula. This Quick Reference section also will refer you to the appropriate sections of the book when you have questions about a particular measure.

The Introduction discusses how to choose and use measures that can help you build a case for supporting your school library media center.

Introduction

Using output measures requires much more than mastering formulas and collecting data. A good understanding of what information each measure conveys, judicious selection of which measures to use, and careful construction of your case are all necessary for presenting convincing data to support a proposal. An overview of the measures and their use can guide your planning.

An Overview of the Measures

There are two major categories of output measures: use measures and availability measures. Use measures are exactly what the name implies: how often the school media center or the resources in the center are used. This includes everything from how many people come to the media center, to how many tables are occupied.

Availability measures relate not only to whether requested materials are available, but also the extent to which the media specialist is available to assist students and teachers and the availability of staff development opportunities.

Use Measures

There are a total of 16 specific measures.

- *Media center use measure:* the amount of time and number of individuals using the media center on a daily, weekly, monthly, or yearly basis. For many to whom you will be reporting these data, how the media center is being used at a given moment is important information to tally as well.

- *Materials use measures:* calculations as to exactly what specific resources are being used within and outside the school media center.

— *Circulation rate* gives the number of resources checked out on a daily, weekly, or monthly basis. This figure can be broken down to reflect specific areas of the collection or individual student and teacher populations.

— *In-library use rate* tallies the number of resources being used within the media center at a specific time. As the name implies these materials do not circulate, but are being used within the library by students and/or teachers.

— *Electronic resources hit rate* calculates the number of times students and teachers use stand-alone or networked electronic resources both within the media center or, if resources are networked to individual classrooms, throughout the school.

— *Online resources success rate* tracks the percentage of successful electronic information searches in relation to the number of overall searches conducted.

— *Turnover rate* provides the average number of times a given item within a collection circulates during the year.

— *Furniture and equipment use rate* estimates the amount of time a piece of furniture or equipment is being used during theschool day.

— *Curriculum support request rate* calculates the number of requests from teachers that deal directly with their need for teaching support. This figure is most helpful when paired with the actual request for resources or services.

Availability Measures

• *Resource availability measures:* calculations designed to reflect the number of materials available for students and teachers.

— *Potential curriculum support rate* measures the collection's potential to support a specific area or areas of an individual school's curriculum.

— *Curriculum support fill rate* figures how effectively the existing collection is supporting a school's curriculum. This measure can be calculated from both the teacher's and the student's perspective.

— *Independent reading/information fill rate*, a student-generated statistic, monitors how well the collection is meeting the leisurereading/activity needs of a student population.

• *School library media specialist availability measures:* All these measures illustrate whether the school library media specialist is available to assist both students and teachers at point of need.

— *Planning opportunity rate* gives the percentage of time a school library media specialist is able to completely fill a teacher's or team's request for assistance in planning a lesson or unit of instruction.

— *Teaching availability measure* provides the percentage of time the school library media specialist is available to work with individuals, small groups, or whole classes at the specific request of a teacher. Daily fixed schedules are not included in this calculation.

— *Troubleshooting request rate* represents any request for assistance in solving an equipment problem.

• *Staff development opportunity measures:* A calculation of the number and kind of staff development opportunities available to an educational community.

— *Staff development request rate* lists the percentage of staff development courses offered compared to those requested by school personnel.

— *Staff development attendance rate* calculates the percentage of staff attending specific staff development opportunities compared to potential participants.

Choosing Measures to Make Your Case

While some of the information needed to calculate these measures is already available — especially if you have an automated circulation system — the majority require planning and effort. Therefore, savvy school library media specialists carefully consider exactly what issues they wish to address and then choose those measures that allow them to make their points most effectively. The chart on page xviii illustrates the relationship between the measures and cases they best support. This does not mean that other measures, if already available or collected simultaneously, cannot strengthen your case. It simply means that these measures best make your argument for these specific typical requests.

Notice that the measures that require the most effort and lead time tend to be those most closely related to the media center program. Many principals also will confide that these measures define the difference between a mediocre media program and a vibrant one. The results garnered from these particular measures often hinge upon the intangible — how a school library media specialist works with teachers and students and the general ambiance of the media center itself.

These particular measures have the potential to tell very different stories depending upon who is doing the storytelling. For instance, very vivacious, conscientious school library media specialists may have high or low curriculum support fill rates. The rate itself means nothing until it is tied to a specific need for information. Is it being used to make the case for additional resources? A low curriculum support fill rate will help lobby for more money to purchase materials. Or is it illustrating the effectiveness of the existing program, a case best represented by documenting a high curriculum support fill rate? The point is, all statistics allow you to manipulate data in very specific ways. Program statistics probably are the most vulnerable to manipulation. *Choose carefully the measures you use to construct your case,*

Figure 1

Measures and What They Support

Supports / Measure	Budget	Flexible Schedule	Planning Time	Staffing	Existing Data	Effort Required[+]	Time Frame
Media Center Use Rate	X	X		X		Medium	Specified
Circ. Rate	X	(X)		X	X*	Low	Specified
In-Library Use Rate	X	X	(X)	X		Medium	Specified
Electronic Resources Hit Rate	X			X	X*	Low	Specified
Online Resources Success Rate	X			X		High	Specified
Turnover Rate	X				X*	Low	Specified
Furniture/ Equipment Use Rate	X	(X)		X		Medium	Specified
Potential Curric. Fill Rate	X		(X)	(X)		High	Specified
Curric. Support Fill Rate	X	(X)	(X)	(X)		High	Specified
Independ. Reading/ Information Fill Rate	X	(X)	(X)	(X)	Survey	High	Specified
Media Specialist Availability Rate		X	X	X	Survey	High	Specified
Planning Opportunity Rate		X	X	X		High	Over time
Teaching Availability Rate		X		X		High	Over time
Troubleshooting Request Rate		X		X		High	Specified or over time
Staff Dev. Request Rate	X	X				Medium	Over time
Staff Dev. Attendance Rate	X	(X)				Low	Specified

* With automated circulation system

[+] Effort required:
    Low – data either already available or easily calculated
    Medium – data can be gathered while media specialist or designee does other tasks; minimum interruption
    High – requires extra time and effort to gather and calculate data

( ) These measures can be used, in concert with those specifically targeted to address a certain issue, to make a stronger case.

remaining fully aware of the potential for any statistic to tell a totally different story from the one planned. Above all, retain your integrity and the integrity of your program during the process. No amount of money, no amount of extra help or flexible schedule, is worth its loss.

How to Use *Output Measures* to Construct Your Case

It is important to remember that the intent of *Output Measures* has never been for the school library media specialist to gather and calculate data for every measure in this book at one time, for one report. Rather, choose the specific measures that will enable you to illustrate your specific need.

Thus, if you are frustrated with your ability to meet the needs of your faculty and students because you are locked into a fixed schedule, you might choose to calculate the media center use rate, in-library use rate, school library media specialist availability rate, planning opportunity rate, and teaching availability rate. Or, you may decide that even these five measures are too many to calculate. In this case, you might choose school library media specialist availability, planning opportunity, and teaching availability measures as the ones with the most potential to prove your premise.

The temptation to choose as few measures as possible to make your case will always exist. The motives here are certainly understandable, but my advice to you is to be sure that you choose enough measures to build a solid case the first time. The last thing you want to have happen is to spend days, weeks, or even months gathering and calculating data, illustrating its relationships, and developing conclusions — only to have a skeptical administrator declare your presentation invalid or inconclusive for lack of solid data. Worse yet would be to go through the above process and end up with the request to provide additional or more complete data before a decision is rendered. Administrators might not understand that the process would be compromised if you were to add March data to statistics originally collected in October, that you would simply have to start over. Likewise, they might not comprehend the effort this data collection and analysis requires of a school library media specialist already stretched to capacity by her "day job." Returning a lengthy report for additional data could be devastating. So do it right the first time.

You can even begin the data collection before you ever decide to make a formal request. Most school library media specialists collect some sort of program statistics, and those of us with automated systems already have a built-in statistical capacity. Therefore, we can— and probably should—begin to observe trends and contemplate possibilities long before we launch a formal proposal blitz.

Once you have decided upon the measures, you can proceed with the actual data gathering and calculation. This book gives you the details on how to do this and guides you through both processes. Tally forms herein are easily and legally replicable, but much of the information ideally relies upon the technology already in place in your media center. Your OPAC (Online Public Access Catalog) will be an invaluable resource as you calculate data, as will front-end counting programs on your CD-ROM stations. The less hand tracking of statistics you do, the lower the margin of error for you—and the lower the possibility of the charge of "cooking the books." Don't despair, however, if you do not have an automated catalog. School library media specialists have been garnering statistics by hand for decades, so simply continue to do so, praising your own diligence (and perhaps looking for measures that can justify an OPAC!). Additionally, many measures must rely upon hand notes — for instance, to calculate the planning opportunity or media specialist availability rates. Unfortunately, these also tend to be those that require the longest lead time to make a substantive case. Accept this fact, take a deep breath, buy a notebook, create a computer file, and begin. The results — more resources to support teaching and learning in your school — are well worth the effort.

Part I

Choosing and Using the Measures

Chapter 1

Use Measures

Use measures are the easiest measures to track and often can be extremely effective in making a case for more staff, higher budgets, and even schedule changes. They can be divided into *media center use measures* and *materials use measures*. These measures, when taken together, give an accurate picture of the overall use of both a facility and its collection.

Both sets of measures can be labor intensive; thus certain generalized suggestions follow:

1. Sample a typical week, ideally one in the fall and one in the spring. These are weeks when you are certain that your statistics will reflect normal media center use. (The week before Christmas vacation would *not* be considered typical!) During this period, make sure that everyone knows that you will be taking the time to gather statistics as accurately as possible. An announcement at a faculty meeting, an informal chat with influential teachers and administrators, letters home to parents, and a written reminder in faculty mailboxes will help gain acceptance and understanding for the process.

2. Enlist volunteers to assist in the count. Elementary school library media specialists may tap the school (or media center's) parent volunteer roster. Middle and high schools more likely will use the student media assistants already in place throughout most of the class day.

3. Don't forget to log before- and afterschool use of the media center by both students and teachers.

4. Make sure counts reflect accurately what is happening in the media center.

Media Center Use Measures

The fourth suggestion above — "Make sure counts reflect accurately what is happening in the media center" — is a particularly important reminder when calculating media center use measures. The subtleties of what actually is happening in your school library information center may go unnoticed if everyone logging the figures isn't attuned to what you are trying to document. For instance, when Mrs. Jones brings in her sixth-grade language arts class, she has brought in 1 LA (language arts) class consisting of 27 students and 1 teacher — tallies in all categories of figure 1-1 except "other." (*Other* is a parent, administrator — someone other than the "expected" clientele.) If, during that same class period, 2 teachers come to check out materials, 4 students arrive to do research for seventh-grade social studies, 2 students come to read magazines, and the principal wanders through on his way to track down an errant student, your total for the period is 1 class, 2 grade levels, 33 students, 3 teachers, 2 subject areas (LA, SS), and 1 other.

Figure 1-1

Sample Daily Tracking Form

	Class	Students	Teachers	Other	Subject	Grade
Before school 7:30 – 8						
1st period 8 – 9	1	27+4+2	1+1+1	1	SS LA	7th 6th
2nd period 9 – 10						
3rd period 10 – 11						
4th period 11 – 12						
lunch 12 – 1						
5th period 1 – 2						
6th period 2 – 3						
After school 3 – 4						

Daily Tracking Form

	Class	Students	Teachers	Other	Subject	Grade
Before school 7:30 – 8						
1st period 8 – 9						
2nd period 9 – 10						
3rd period 10 – 11						
4th period 11 – 12						
lunch 12 – 1						
5th period 1 – 2						
6th period 2 – 3						
After school 3 – 4						

Figure 1-2

Sample Weekly Media Center Use Analysis

Student Body: 625
Teachers: 22

1. Total number of classes visiting media center	38
2. Total number of students (during school day)	1,448
Total number of students (before/after school)	129
	1,577
3. Total number of teachers (during school day)	27
Total number of teachers (before/after school)	33
4. Other (parents, administrators, etc.)	87
5. Subjects	6 LA
	12 SS
	2 Math
	14 Health
	2 Science
6. Grade Level	12 sixth
	13 seventh
	13 eighth

Highest use day: Monday
Highest use time: 10 – 11
Lowest use day: Friday
Lowest use time: 2 – 3

How to Analyze and Use the Data

1. From Figure 1-2, you can derive that, in the above school, you have slightly more than one class using the media center each period of the day (38 divided by 5 = 7.6 / 6 periods each day / 5 days each week). Stated another way, 5% of your classes are using the media center at any given time during the school day. That's heavy use!

2. A total of 1,577 students used the media center during the week. This works out to approximately 315 students per day, or half the 625 member student body visiting the media center daily — again, *very* heavy use.

3. Since use figures indicate heavy use in mornings and at the beginning of the week, a case can be made for part-time assistant help at one of the following times: every morning, all day Monday through Wednesday, or Monday through Thursday mornings.

Hot Spots! (possible implications from the data)

• Note the small number of teachers using the media center when compared to the number of students using media center. If only 27 teachers visit the media center during the same week, there *might* be a problem with teacher support of the media program. The media center might be a dumping ground for teacher planning time.

• While grade-level use appears equal for this specific week, subject use is not. This may impact collection development in both Social Studies and Health Education areas especially, although more detailed materials use records would be warranted.

The Measure at a Glance

Use **media center use measures** to request more staff, budget increases, or schedule changes.

Use the tracking form on page 5 to collect data, and then follow these patterns to calculate the measures that will support your case:

$$\text{\# classes per day using media center} = \frac{\text{\# class visits}}{5 \text{ (or other \# of days in sample)}}$$

$$\text{\# classes per period using media center} = \frac{\text{\# classes per day}}{\text{\# periods in school day}}$$

$$\text{\# students per day using media center} = \frac{\text{\# student visits}}{5 \text{ (or other \# of days in sample)}}$$

$$\text{\# students per period using media center} = \frac{\text{\# students per day}}{\text{\# periods in school day}}$$

For an example of how these measures can be used, read "The Case for a Technology Assistant" (pages 71 – 78) to see how Paul collects and organizes media center use measures to support his proposal for a technology assistant.

Materials Use Measures

Materials use measures are similar throughout library literature: *circulation*, *in-library use*, and *turnover rate*. Two less traditional use measures are more related to school media centers, however: *furniture and equipment use* and the *curriculum support request rate*. Though all can be collected during the designated weeks for statistical gathering, the curriculum support request rate would be more accurate if monitored for an entire year.

Circulation of Materials

Four different categories of circulation data — *student circulation rate*, *teacher circulation rate*, *subject area circulation rate*, and *grade level circulation rate* — can be gathered by one sampling. Additionally, media centers with automated circulation systems can give an even more accurate count by using the accumulated data collected throughout the school year. Whether collected during the sample week or throughout the school year, circulation statistics are a quick means of calculating a collection's use. Simply divide the number of students within your school into the total number of materials circulated to students throughout the year (or sample period). Voila! Your student circulation rate. Likewise, for teachers. Subject area and grade level circulation can be determined if desired.

Note the following:

- Renewals are counted within the circulation rate.
- All materials that circulate within a patron group should be counted. For example, if teachers check out AV, computer software, kits, *and* books, statistics should be kept in all categories. Depending on the information presented, circulation can be logged together or separated into individual formats.

If you are not lucky enough to have an automated circulation system, tallies for the week (or the year) can be made similar to the manner in which media center use statistics were logged. *Warning: the longer statistics are kept manually, the less accurate they tend to be simply because it is so difficult to remain consistent over weeks and months.* Thus, in the same 625-student, 22-teacher middle school we examined for media center use statistics, the following circulation data can be derived:

Figure 1-3

Sample Circulation Measures

Student Circulation

Books: $\dfrac{20{,}872}{625}$ = 33.4 books/student/year

Teacher Circulation

Books: $\dfrac{1{,}237}{22}$ = 56.2 books/teacher/year

AV: $\dfrac{210}{22}$ = 9.5 AV/teacher/year

Software: $\dfrac{71}{22}$ = 3.2 software/teacher/year

Teacher circulation can be broken down even further into circulation within the professional collection and the regular collection, and teacher and student circulation could be broken down into more specific areas of the collection. For instance, in elementary schools, distinguish between circulation of easy and fiction materials, and Dewey categories of nonfiction.

How to Analyze and Use the Data

- The circulation rate according to grade level can be an eye-opening statistic. If sixth and seventh graders account for the majority of circulations of materials, a perceptive school library media specialist may do well to ask what to do to encourage materials use with the school's eighth grade students and teachers. A note of caution, however: Combining circulation rate and in-library use rate (see the next section) gives a more accurate picture of a media center's materials use rate than does either statistic alone.

- Comparing circulation rates before and after certain programs are introduced can be particularly effective. For instance, circulation rates before and after a sustained silent reading program is imple-

The Measure at a Glance

Use **circulation of materials measures** in combination with other measures such as in-library use rate to build a stronger argument for an increased budget. Among the many uses for these statistics are assessing each grade's use of the center, studying the effect new curricular units have on circulation, or requesting staff assistance.

Collect your data carefully and consistently throughout the tracking period, and then follow this pattern to calculate the measures that will support your case:

$$\text{Circulation rate per student or teacher} = \frac{\text{\# items circulated per year}}{\text{\# students or teachers}}$$

Use the other materials use measures in this chapter to address specific uses of media center materials.

mented in a school may justify an increase in the book budget. A low software checkout may mean that, in spite of a new computer in each teacher's classroom, little curricular use is being made of the technology. A savvy school library media specialist might use these statistics to justify staff development for her teachers in the area of how to integrate certain software packages into the curriculum. Particularly high circulation of environmental materials may indicate that the schoolwide ecology emphasis is successful and that the school may wish to funnel more resources into these areas of the collection — or target additional topics for whole-school initiatives.

• Justification for media assistance can be made by using student circulation figures. If the yearly circulation is 20,872 books in the student category, this works out to an average of 118 books per day (20,872 divided by 180 school days = 118 books/day). Although this statistic alone probably would not convince any principal to hire even a part-time assistant, were it combined with other data such as in-library use, teaching availability, and planning opportunity rates, this circulation rate might be significant.

In-Library Use Rate

The in-library use rate gives the number of resources being used within the school library media center at a specific time. These materials were not checked out during any particular period/day, but were being used in the library by students and/or teachers. This statistic can be time-consuming and difficult to tally, but it can be one of the most useful when justifying staff or budget numbers. High in-center use rates can indicate exciting, innovative programming. Conversely, high in-center use may pinpoint problems with a school's overall educational philosophy, especially if it views the library media program as a baby-sitting service or for teacher planning time only. One word of caution here: as more and more resources are networked into individual classrooms, savvy school library media specialists make sure that their file servers are configured to track hit rates for each networked program so that the use of these resources is reflected somewhere in the overall statistical report (see the section on electronic resources hit rate for further information).

The actual process for collecting these data is a simple one: count up all the resources that are used within the media center during a single class period or a single school day. When setting up the data collection process for in-center use, there are some procedures you would do well to implement:

• No one (users or staff) shelves anything until it has been tallied. Make sure that you (and your volunteers) are prepared to log in the various measure indicators, help students complete assignments, straighten up, and be ready for the next class — all at the same time.

• Can data for calculating other measures be gathered at the same time? Some of these measures involve redundancy. In-center use of computers or networked resources could be tallied as furniture/equipment use as well. You may use the information in different ways, but it certainly can be gathered at the same time.

- Separate in-center use statistics can be logged for students and teachers, although this is not as important here as in circulation rate or media center use. If space or equipment availability is an issue, however — for instance, if teachers are lobbying for a computer in their own rooms or you are lobbying for a special professional collection area within your media center or the school — then this segregation of data makes sense.

- Materials can be broken down into more specific categories — books into reference, fiction, nonfiction, easy; networked resources into individual products like *Information Finder*, *SIRS*, and *Newsbank*; magazines into research and pleasure. (Be careful with the research vs. pleasure magazine data! Some well-meaning educators and parents do not believe that leisure-reading magazines are a justifiable school expense.)

So in our 625-member middle school that was tracking the in-library use rate of both books and CD-ROMs, the calculations might look like this:

1,572 books/week x 36 weeks/year =

$$\frac{56,592 \text{ books/year}}{625 \text{ students}} = 90.5 \text{ books/student/year}$$

How To Analyze and Use the Data

- Circulating 90.5 books/student/year is heavy use according to anyone's definition and ought to be justification for budget and/or staff increases. Do not assume, however, that the public will understand the magnitude of this statistic. Take care to place figures like this into a context that others can relate to. For instance, the South-

---

The Measure at a Glance

Use the **in-library use** statistics to justify a budget increase, reallocation of funds, or additional staff.

Use the suggestions on pages 9 –11 to collect data, and then follow this pattern to calculate the measures that will support your case:

$$\text{In-library use rate} = \frac{\text{\# items used in media center}}{\text{\# of students enrolled} + \text{ teachers}}$$

Don't forget to collect data for use of online sources or CD-ROMs.

ern Association of Colleges and Schools (SACS) recommends 10 books per student in a media center collection — and your students are using 90.5 books/person/year in the media center alone! Add to this the circulation figures of 33.4 books/students/year and you have student overall use of nearly 1 book per school day per year. That ought to impress anyone!

Consider other hypothetical in-library use statistics:

52 students/6 period day at 1 CD-ROM workstation =
8.7 students/period/day

- If you are averaging more than 6 students each period at a single-station CD-ROM — really about all that can take advantage of a CD-ROM during the hour, since that is less than 10 minutes per search — you have a strong case for adding additional, networked search stations.

63 students/day/periodical pleasure reading vs.
8 students/day/periodical research

- If students are indicating heavy use of magazines for pleasure reading as opposed to research, two scenarios may be developing:
  - CD-ROM full-text magazines may have replaced the research format; you may want to cut some of these particular magazine subscriptions.
  - The media center is being used for more than curricular activities. This statistic has pros and cons, so use it as you see fit.

Interestingly enough, statistics like this may push you toward more in-class use of materials. If these statistics reflect a chaotic media center, you may wish to put together research materials to be sent to a teacher's room, thus cutting down on in-center use but, conversely, increasing circulation figures or the networked electronic resources hit rate.

Electronic Resources Hit Rate

The electronic resources hit rate calculates the number of times students and teachers use stand-alone or networked electronic resources both within the media center or, if the resources are networked to individual classrooms, throughout the school. Single-station and networked computers can be programmed to keep track of the number of times they are used. This is particularly helpful in justifying the shift in budget from print to nonprint (or vice versa). These statistics can be cumulative or programmed for a specific time frame, depending on your particular need. Consult your software vendor or school technology specialist for help in programming your computer to collect these data; printing it out at the end of each class period, hour, or day; and analyzing it at a later date.

How to Analyze and Use the Data

Although the number of times students and teachers use electronic resources is interesting, straightforward information, it can be particularly effective to combine them with other access and use measures to combat a climate of downsizing in which the building-level school library media specialist is deemed nonessential. For instance, if media center use and circulation measures decline after the CD-ROM encyclopedia is networked to the classrooms, an astute school library media specialist will begin to ask, "How can the teacher and students in those classrooms get all the information they need if they are only using that encyclopedia? How can I convince teachers that there is equally important information in other resources here in the media center?"

As more and more resources are being networked to the classroom, a perceptive school library media specialist also will see her area of operation moving from the media center to the classroom. Information skills still need to be *taught* regardless of where they are *used*. The logical teaching team continues to be both teacher and media specialist; only the venue changes. Of course, this opens another can of worms. If the school library media specialist is in the classroom, then it becomes imperative that the schedule be flexible and that a media assistant be in the library. These statistics become fodder for that justification.

The Measure at a Glance

Use the **electronic resources hit rate** to justify a shift in budget from print to nonprint or vice versa, or with other access and use measures to update the media specialist's job description for the technological age and defend your position.

There is no formula here because the rates will be taken from your system's tracking program.

Consult your software vendor or school technology specialist about programming your computer to record the necessary data. Once you have gathered the data, you may want to refer to the in-library use discussion for analysis and data use suggestions.

Turnover Rate

The turnover rate of a collection is the average number of times a given item within a collection circulates during the year. Again, an automated circulation system allows for easy calculation of this statistic, one that is figured by dividing the number of materials circulated annually by the number of items in the collection. Thus, in our 625-member middle school that had a circulation rate of 20,872 books per year and an in-library use rate of 56,692 books per year out of a total book collection of 18,000 books, the turnover rate of the collection would be 4.3. In other words, each item in the book collection is circulated an average of 4.3 times per year — definitely a high turnover rate!

$$20{,}872 + 56{,}692 = \frac{77{,}564 \text{ books}}{18{,}000 \text{ total books in the collection}}$$

$$= 4.3 \text{ turnover rate}$$

The Measure at a Glance

Use the **turnover rate** in conjunction with the materials access measures to see how the availability of materials affects the turnover rate; to justify an increase in the materials budget, particularly for targeted portions of the collection; to justify allocation of funds for print or electronic resources; or to request additional staff.

If you have an automated circulation system, this measure will be easy to determine. If your system is not yet automated, you will have to track circulation very carefully. This measure is most persuasive if you combine both circulation and counts of in-library use of materials. Once you have the data, follow this pattern to determine your turnover rate:

$$\text{Turnover rate} = \frac{\text{\# circulations and uses (include in-library use if possible)}}{\text{\# items in collection}}$$

Consider the following before you tackle turnover rate:

1. Turnover rate can be calculated accurately only if a collection is weeded consistently. A collection containing too many materials that are out-of-date or unattractive will result in a low turnover rate.

2. Although some schools, particularly middle and high schools, may decide to include in-library use rates as part of the total figure used to calculate turnover rate, at times they may wish to determine the turnover rate for one particular section of the collection. For instance, the reference collection turnover rate in a high school would depend almost entirely upon in-library use figures, whereas the picture book turnover rate in an elementary school would focus on checked-out materials.

3. Occasionally, especially if a collection is not yet automated, some items will not be figured into a collection count — for instance, paperbacks. The irony is that sometimes these are the very items with high circulation rates. Thus, if these items figure into your circulation statistics, they must also be added to your total collection count.

How to Analyze and Use the Data

- Compare the turnover rate of your collection with some of the access measures. Often, a high turnover rate is synonymous with a low materials availability measure — when materials are in circulation, they cannot be accessed by someone else.

- A high turnover rate can be used to justify an increase in the materials budget. Targeting figures for one portion of the collection — the picture books, AV, software, science books — often can help funders understand the need for an infusion of money into the media program.

- Turnover rates can help you make the hard decisions. Calculating the turnover rate of certain reference books like the encyclopedias — in spite of the availability of a CD-ROM encyclopedia — can help you decide whether to continue the purchase of all five encyclopedia sets or to justify several more networked computer workstations.

- High turnover rates can substantiate the need for a media assistant, a second school library media specialist, student assistants, or more parent volunteers.

Furniture and Equipment Use Rate

Not enough CD-ROM workstations in your media center? Are there enough tables and chairs for whole-class instruction and other students doing reference work at the same time? Do students consistently stand in line to use the automated catalog? If any of these scenarios sound familiar, calculating the furniture and equipment use rate may help you solve that problem.

The furniture and equipment use rate is the amount of time a piece of furniture or equipment is being used during the school day. Take, care to include before- and afterschool use, as well as lunchtime and study halls. As a matter of fact, high schools may find that furniture and equipment use rates are especially important when justifying additional staffing or (unfortunately) when a school library media specialist must argue the closing of the center to unassigned traffic during lunch.

When setting up to gather furniture and equipment use rates, take into consideration the following:

1. Choose a finite period of time for gathering data. A week during the fall and a week during the spring should give a fairly accurate picture of use, although a smart school library media specialist might choose term paper or project week if it is possible to count and serve student needs simultaneously. Choose a specific time each period or hour — say, ten minutes into the class — to walk through the media center recording furniture or equipment use.

2. Traditionally, furniture and equipment use rates calculate only the number of facilities/workstations used, not the number of children at a single computer. In schools, however, this method of calculation may not provide the data a school library media specialist needs since two or more children may be working at a computer because there are not enough workstations to go around. Or they may be completing a group assignment and only need the one station. How you report it is your judgment call. If you want to justify additional workstations, calculate each workstation use separately — for example, 3 children using 1 workstation provides a use rate of 3, or 300%. If 4 students are waiting in line to use the automated catalog, then calculate the use of that piece of equipment as:

   4 students waiting + 1 student using equipment =

   5, or 500% use rate

3. You can be as general or as specific as you need to be in determining the furniture and equipment use rate. Some school library media specialists calculate only the use rate for all the computers in the center; others label each, such as CD-ROM 1, CD-ROM 2, Internet Station 1, Internet Station 2, OPAC 1, OPAC 2. You even can calculate specific areas of the facility — the reference or leisure reading furniture or the computer lab stations.

4. This next variation is complicated, but may be necessary when trying to convey overcrowded conditions to administrators. It involves logging in every person who uses a piece of equipment during a single class period. Obviously, a single school library media specialist will find this impossible. Student assistants or parent volunteers are a must if this particular measure is to be calculated accurately and sanely.

How to Analyze and Use the Data

The application of furniture and equipment use rates has been implied throughout the considerations above. Additional space, more equipment or furniture, further staffing — all can be supported by furniture and equipment use rates. A dose of reality is necessary here, however: librarians like to use furniture and equipment use rates to justify more space. While the administration may be justly impressed and sympathetic to our plight, fiscal realities may not allow for the expansion or construction of a new facility. Thus, the perceptive school library media specialist uses the same information to argue for additional staffing to help deal with student needs and discipline, or even networked computers in each classroom so that students and teachers still have access to electronic resources while leaving the media center free for

The Measure at a Glance

Use the **furniture and equipment use rate** to request more equipment or furniture, further staffing, or even more space if it is feasible.

Use the information on pages 15 – 17 to plan your data collection, and then use the following pattern to calculate the measures that will support your case:

$$\text{Furniture and equipment use rate} = \text{\# students using} + \text{\# students waiting to use item}$$

To express as a percentage, multiply by 100%.

For a more impressive presentation of your needs, present your overall furniture and equipment rate for any given type of equipment. For example, to calculate for all PCs in your media center, follow this pattern:

$$\text{Furniture and equipment use rate} = \frac{\text{total \# students using and waiting to use equipment}}{\text{\# of pieces of equipment}}$$

To express as a percentage, multiply by 100%.

additional research and curricular explorations.

Curriculum Support Request Rate

How many times during the school day do teachers ask you to help them? How often do they send groups of students to the media center for research? How many times a week do you pull materials to send to a classroom or to hold for student research? These tasks are incorporated in the curriculum support request rate — the number of requests from teachers that deal directly with their need for teaching support.

There are two ways to calculate this measure — one a quick snapshot, the other more complex. The idea is to jot down, over a certain length of time, those requests that deal directly with teachers' need for curriculum support. If you find yourself telling teachers that you cannot accommodate their classes in the media center because two other classes are already scheduled, if you find yourself working later than anyone else in the building because you *still* haven't pulled Ms. Burns's biology materials, or if the school library media specialists across the district are being threatened with job loss, then you may need to calculate your curriculum support request rate.

The snapshot data gathering is a simple calculation of the number of times a day teachers ask you to do something that relates to their ability to teach their curriculum. If, over a week's time, you have 33 requests from teachers, then you are averaging 6.6 requests for curriculum support daily.

Figure 1-4

Sample Data Form for Curriculum Support Request Rate

	Request	Time Spent	Outcome
Before school	• Ms. Jones wanted 2 videos for 1st period.	• 5 minutes	• Pulled.
	• Mr. Hoggard wanted to schedule his 3rd period SS class to learn how to use Groliers.	• 5 minutes	• Already teaching 3rd period. Rescheduled for Thurs. 3rd period.
	• Ms. Smith wanted me to help students create PowerPoint presentation in her classroom	• 5 minutes	• Compromised — her students will come here over next week. Can't leave library.
1st period	• Ms. Downs sent 24 students to check out books.	• 45 minutes	• None — just lots of kids in here!
	• Taught 6 students from Ms. Deal's LA class how to use DISCovering Authors.	• 25 minutes	• 6 more students can use DA — and can help teach others.

The problem with this method is that it really doesn't tell us a lot. A more detailed record is far more valuable, particularly if you're trying to justify such things as flexible scheduling, additional staff, or your own job! Consequently, consider using the format in Figure 1-4. A word of advice, however: Curriculum support request rate is best tallied at the same time you are calculating the troubleshooting request rate and/or many of the teacher-specific access measures detailed in Chapter 2.

How to Analyze and Use the Data

• Not all consequences are negative. Having six more students proficient at searching DISCovering Authors is exciting; helping Ms. Jones find her two videos is expected, nothing more, nothing less. But the request to visit the classroom is one for reflection. How much more efficient — not to mention educationally sound — would it have

Use the **curriculum support request rate** to suggest hiring more staff, to propose flexible scheduling, and to modify your schedule to include visits to classrooms. This measure is best tallied at the same time you are working on your troubleshooting request rate or access measures (Chapter 2).

Use the Figure 1.4, Sample Data Form for Curriculum Support Request Rate on page 18 as a guide to collecting data, and then follow this pattern to calculate the measures that will support your case:

$$\text{Curriculum support request rate} = \frac{\text{\# requests from teachers in a week}}{\text{\# teachers}}$$

You can also express this as a daily rate by dividing the number of requests per week by five.

For an example of how these measures can be used, read "The Case for a Technology Assistant" to see why the curriculum support request rate is part of Paul's request for a technical assistant.

been to go to Ms. Smith's classroom and work, uninterrupted, with her and her students on the computers that they would use for their presentations? This might be fodder for staffing justification!

• Curriculum support request rate is more anecdotal in nature than other use measures — more qualitative than quantitative research, you might say. But it can provide quantitative data. How many times during the school day — or week — do you have to refuse or put off supporting a teacher's request because you are dealing with a fixed schedule of back-to-back classes? Can you make a case for flexible scheduling? How many times would it be more efficient and educationally effective for you to move throughout the building for planning or teaching purposes? How many requests must you postpone because you already have too many students in the media center? Additional staffing, even part-time, might be the answer here.

• This use measure goes hand-in-hand with several access measures all detailed in Chapter 2:
    — teacher potential curriculum support rate
    — teacher curriculum support fill rate
    — teaching availability measures
    — media specialist availability measures.

Chapter 2

Access Measures: Resource Availability Measures

Public libraries calculate materials availability by surveying for title, subject, author, and browser fill rates — and certainly schools could learn a great deal from surveys that determine these figures. School library media centers will make better use of their energies, however, by concentrating on measures that directly affect their programs: the potential curriculum support rate for teachers, the independent reading/information support fill rate for students, and the curriculum support fill rate for both teachers and students.

Potential Curriculum Support Rate

The potential curriculum support rate measures the collection's potential to support an individual school's curriculum. The process itself can be a mammoth undertaking if one decides to survey the entire collection and match it with the whole school's curriculum. It can be very manageable, however, if you calculate only one area for a particular grade level or subject.

In essence, the potential curriculum support rate determines the extent to which your collection (or a specific area of your collection) can meet teachers' needs if and when they decide to teach particular units. For instance, your fourth-grade teachers want to do a major unit on weather. After examining your collection, you determine that you have 58 fiction and nonfiction books on weather, 3 videotapes, 2 science periodicals, 3 electronic resources, and 2 teacher activity books in the professional collection that provide weather-related activities and information. You conclude that you probably have enough resources to support the fourth-grade weather unit, or 100% potential curriculum support rate. If, however, you are dealing with a tenth-grade world literature unit on Russian writers and have only 15 books, 1 videotape, 0 periodicals, 2 electronic resources, and 3 professional resources, your potential curriculum support rate is 60%.

How were the percentages determined? While no national standards exist to offer specific numbers for specific units of instruction, certain assumptions given in Figure 2-1 are valid in ascertaining the potential curriculum support fill rate. Be forewarned that these figures and percentages are arbitrary — something an astute administrator probably will point out. They are hardly excessive, however, and points of general reference assist your good decision making. They should be considered benchmarks for comparison and are based upon more than 15 years of working with school media collections. Using the figures in Figure 2-1, we can determine the rates in Figure 2-2.

Figure 2-1

Minimum Curricular Unit Materials for a Single Class

Material Type	Elementary Number	Secondary Number	Percentage
Books (ref/fic/non)	2/student in class (25 in class)	1/student in class (25 in class)	20%
AV	1	1	20%
Periodicals	2 (or 1 full-text CD-ROM with at least 4 subject related periodicals)	4	20%
Electronic resources (not CD-ROM periodicals)	1 encyclopedia; 1 subject related and/or 1 Internet station/class	1 encyclopedia; 1 subject related and/or Internet station/class	20% (10% ency/ 10% CD/I'net)
Professional Collection	1	1	20%

If you want to figure out the percentage of needed *books* you have, divide the number of *books* you have in the collection on this topic by the number of books you need for the unit. You have already decided that books will be 20 percent of all materials for this unit, so multiply the quotient by 20% (.20). The formula is on page 24.

The column labeled percentage is the percentage of all curricular materials that you want from a given category; in the case of the weather unit, 20% of your curricular support for the unit will come from books. Your actual column cannot be a higher number than you have in the percentage column. So for the weather unit, you need 50 books and you have 58, more than enough. Your actual is still 20% because you are not going to rely on books for more than 20% of your support materials.

Figure 2-2

Potential Curriculum Support Rate

Elementary

Date: 2/24/98
Topic: Weather
Teacher/Grade Level: 4
Date to be implemented: 4/8/98

Resource	Adequate	Actual	Percentage/Actual	
Books (ref/fic/non)	2/student	58	20%	20%
AV	1	3	20%	20%
Periodicals (includes full-text databases)	2	2	20%	20%
Electronic resources (not periodicals)	1 encyclopedia 1 subject-related and/or 1 Internet station/class	3	20%	20%
Professional collection	1	2	20%	20%
			100%	100%

Secondary

Date: 2/24/98
Topic: Russian Writers
Teacher/Grade Level: 10
Date to be implemented: 3/11/98

Resource	Adequate	Actual	Percentage/Actual	
Books (ref/fic/non)	1/student	15	20%	129%
AV	1	1	20%	20%
Periodicals (includes full-text databases)	4	0	20%	0%
Electronic resources (not CD-ROM periodicals)	1 encyclopedia; 1 subject-related and/or 1 Internet station/class	2	20%	20%
Professional collection	1	3	20%	20%
			100%	72%

The Measure at a Glance

Use the **potential curriculum support rate** to determine whether the collection can support a new unit of instruction and to request budget supplements or reallocation of funds if necessary.

Use the model charts and the instructions on pages 21 – 23 to collect data, and then follow this pattern to calculate the measures that will support your case:

$$\text{Potential curriculum support rate} = \frac{\text{\# items available in collection}}{\text{\# items needed for unit or course}} \times .20 \text{ (or 20\%)}$$

Note:

This rate is predicated on the assumption that 20% of curricular support from each of five formats: books, audiovisual, periodicals, electronic resources, professional collection — adjust the .20 multiplier as appropriate for your situation.

For an example of how the potential curriculum support rate can be used, read "The Case for Collection Development before New Course Addition" where Katrina and Carlos use this measure to determine the extent to which they can support some proposed new courses and suggest a time frame for introducing the courses into the curriculum.

How to Analyze and Use the Data

- The potential curriculum support rate is most effective when determining whether a collection will be able to support a new unit of instruction. As a new curriculum evolves, one of the major questions that should be asked before it is implemented is whether sufficient resources exist to enable teachers to teach it effectively and efficiently. By looking at the potential curriculum support rate, media specialists can justify budget supplements or, if that is impossible, a diversion of resources from other subject/unit area budgets, at least for the short run.

- Augment the potential curriculum support rate by compiling bibliographies of the actual titles that represent these numbers. This will enable teachers (and you!) to know exactly what is in the collection on a particular topic. Once this information is made available, you should see better use of the existing collection.

Hot Spots!

- Unweeded collections make all numbers invalid! If materials are too outdated, inaccurate, and unattractive to be used, they should not be considered as potentially supporting the curriculum.

- If a whole school or grade level does a unit at the same time, some of these numbers are invalid too. Multiply each category of books by two-thirds the total number of students using them at the same time. For example, if all 4 fourth grades teach the weather unit simultaneously and each class averages 25 students, the library information center would need 130 books on weather. Likewise, it would need 3 professional resources. The more general resources — AV, periodicals, and electronic resources — can be shared; more would be helpful, but they are not necessary for implementation of the program.

- For some units (e.g., Russian Writers), it is unrealistic to expect periodicals focusing on this information to be part of a school collection. Thus, another judgment call is in order: a subscription or access to *Humanities* or perhaps the *New York Times Book Review* would be counted, as would a subscription to *Electric Library*, as the full 20 percent. Or an N/A could be logged in that particular column and 25 percent used as your base percentage.

- If only one teacher teaches the unit, the numbers themselves are still valid, but you may have a hard time justifying the expenditures. Possible solution: See if you can find multiple uses for these resources.

Curriculum Support Fill Rate

The method for collecting this information is identical for both teacher and student. Essentially, curriculum support fill rate calculates how effectively your collection is supporting your school's curriculum, first in the eyes of your teachers and then in the eyes of your students. Unfortunately, unlike all the other measures discussed, curriculum support fill rate (and independent reading/information support fill rate and online resources success rate) requires that both teachers and students provide the information needed to calculate these measures, usually through individual surveys (see the section Surveying Your Teachers and Students).

To calculate your curriculum support fill rate, divide the number of actual requests or searches for materials by the number of materials found. For example, if a faculty member is searching for a teacher activity book on weather and finds it, the curriculum support fill rate for that particular transaction is 100 percent. If, however, she is looking for five books on hurricanes to share with her class and your library information center has three that she considers appropriate, the curriculum support fill rate would be 60 percent. The same process would be used for students. If a middle-school student was completing a research assignment on Vietnam for which he needed at least five sources — two books, one magazine article, one encyclopedia article, and one other reference source — and he found all except the "other" reference source, the curriculum support fill rate for this transaction would be 80 percent.

Curriculum support fill rate can be calculated by individual transactions as above or by totaling all transactions over a designated time period (see Calculating the Results). Both provide usable but very different information.

A warning: One of the most frustrating aspects of calculating the curriculum support fill rate is the caveat that if a teacher or student says that the library doesn't have what they need — even if you know that resources were available that they, technically, could have used — the search was not successful in their eyes and the curriculum support fill rate will reflect this perception. Consequently, the more assistance we can offer our patrons, the more accurate will be our curriculum support fill rate (not to mention our overall PR rating as well!).

Hot Spots!

- Schools with poor library media center staffing probably will have lower curriculum support fill rates.

- Likewise, poor collections should produce low curriculum support fill rates, although this is not always the case. Students and teachers often will opt for something old, basically inaccurate, or inadequate simply to complete an assignment or lesson. *Make sure that your collection is weeded so that it reflects this rate legitimately.*

- Middle- and high-school media specialists inevitably will have some problems with pranksters who fill out forms with a variety of inaccurate or irrelevant (and irreverent) responses. Thus, some libraries will choose to calculate a *response rate*: the percentage of usable reponses as compared to the actual number of responses (see page 23). Although an excellent technique, a more practical method for some schools may be targeted dissemination; choose who will get surveys and when. For instance, a whole class surveyed under teacher guidance or a one-on-one conversation with a student whom you have just helped is likely to provide useful information and statistics. Some might argue that this "stacks the deck," but I prefer to believe that it will provide feedback that will more accurately reflect the status of our collections.

The Measure
at a Glance

Use the **curriculum support fill rate** to assess teacher and student perceptions of how well the media center is supporting the school curriculum. It is useful for developing the collection, requesting larger budgets or specific budgeted items, requesting additional staff, or implementing better service procedures.

Use the survey forms on pages 31 – 34 to collect data, and then follow this pattern to calculate your support fill rate:

$$\text{Curriculum support fill rate} = \frac{\text{\# appropriate curriculum-related materials found in collection}}{\text{\# items sought by teachers and/ or students for coursework}}$$

For an example of how this can be used, read "The Case for Flexible Access," in which Mary uses the curriculum support fill rate to show that her need to give more time to student requests argues in favor of flexible scheduling.

Independent Reading/Information Fill Rate

The independent reading/information fill rate is a student-generated statistic similar to the browsing rate in public library materials access surveys. Again, it is calculated by the number of materials/activities found, divided by the number of materials/activities sought. Thus, if a student comes in looking for *Hatchet* by Gary Paulsen and a copy is on the shelf, this would be indicated on the form as a 100 percent fill rate for this transaction. If all copies are checked out, however, the search would have been unsuccessful, a 0 percent fill rate. Media center activities can also be part of the independent reading/information fill rate. Consequently, if two or three students enter the center during lunch to read magazines or play chess, their activities would be indicated on the survey as well (see Surveying Your Teachers and Students for actual forms).

Hot Spots!

- Many students will not want to fill in specific title or subject lines. Solution: Provide a browsing category on the survey for privacy.

- Some school library media specialists will see this form as unnecessary if they are using the student curriculum support fill rate. Indeed, you can use that form for both, thereby simplifying data collection.

The Measure at a Glance

Use the **independent reading/information fill rate** to supplement data from the curriculum support fill rate. These statistics represent students' satisfaction with their use of the media center for information or activities other than class work.

Use the survey form on page 33 to collect data, and then follow this pattern to calculate your independent reading/information fill rate:

$$\text{Independent reading/information fill rate} = \frac{\text{\# items found}}{\text{\# items sought by students}}$$

For an example of how to use this measure, read "The Case for Flexible Access." In making her proposal for flexible scheduling, Mary combines the independent reading/information fill rate with the curriculum support fill rate to present a more comprehensive measure of service to students.

Surveying Your Teachers and Students

Resource access surveys are fairly straightforward and easy to create. They simply ask how successful were teachers and/or students (or, in the case of the potential curriculum support rate, how successful teachers would be) in their searches for information. See pages 31 – 33 for ready-to-use survey forms.

Administering the Survey

- Decide whether to distribute the surveys to everyone and calculate the response rate or to target individual students and teachers to receive them.
- Determine the time frame for the surveys. One week in the fall and/ or one week in the spring should give adequate information for collection development provided you maintain a constant dialogue with teachers throughout the year. It is wise to give adequate survey lead time so that the results can be used when ordering materials.
- You may want to keep teacher curriculum support fill rate sheets available throughout the school year so that teachers can provide ongoing input for future collection development use. (You may wish to do a less formal Suggestion Box for student requests throughout the year.)
- Calculate the potential curriculum support rate as soon as possible after being notified of changing curriculum, so that resources can be budgeted for and ordered before the next school year.

Each form includes a space for a number so that you can track how many forms have been distributed and how many returned. This is particularly important if you are calculating the response rate.

Calculating the Results

- Create a tabulation form — one for teachers and one for students — that helps you easily calculate fill rates:

Figure 2-3

Sample Student Curriculum Support Fill Rate Data

Form Number	Subject Sought	Subject Found
1	3	3
2	1	0
3	1	1
4	5	2
5	1	1
Total	11	7

Student curriculum support fill rate:
    64% [divide number found (7) by number sought (11)]

- Do not tally results unless both the Subject Sought and Subject Found columns are completed. Counting items sought without placing a value in the found column as well will skew the results.

• Do not count responses from any surveys that are unclear or incomplete. Use this information for the response rate only (if you are tallying response rate).

Figure 2-4

Sample Survey Response Rate Data

Surveys distributed:	95
Surveys returned with usable information:	89
Survey Response Rate:	93.7%

[Number returned (89) divided by number distributed (95)]

• Create another form for collection development purposes. (Use form on page 34.)

Collection Development Form

Subjects/Activities Not Found	Number of Times Sought
1.	
2.	
3.	

How to Analyze and Use the Data

• Obviously, the first use of this data is for your own collection development needs. Here in a nutshell is what your teachers and students are looking for in your school library media center — and what they are finding.

• Beyond this, use these figures to justify larger budgets or specific budgeted items. If students are having only a 25% fill rate on electronic resources, you have ample evidence that you need either more CD-ROM titles or additional CD-ROM or Internet workstations.

• Analyze the subjects not found. If you *know* that these materials are in your media center, then you may have ammunition to justify additional staff — or you may need to examine how existing staff provides service!

• Sometimes the most useful information is found in the comment lines at the bottom of the surveys. Both teachers and students can provide some surprising insights into the media program when given the opportunity. Put aside your feelings and read the comments objectively, learning from the valid suggestions and sloughing off the illegitimate claims (sometimes easier said than done!).

• Speaking of usable information: Calculating the curriculum support fill rate is an interesting exercise that might yield some statistics that can be referred to quickly and easily. But the best information is on the individual sheets which tell you the subjects sought and found. If you have time, calculate the actual percentage of fill rate to see how you're doing or if you see consistently low numbers, but spend the majority of your energies analyzing the raw data.

Hot Spots! Collections with low turnover rates may have very high curriculum support fill rates and independent reading/information fill rates for obvious reasons — and vice versa. Consider use measures as you examine fill rates! Neither is informative in isolation.

Teacher Curriculum Support Fill Rate

Please complete the information below, indicating the specific information you were searching for in the media center and whether you found that information. Thank You!

Number: _____

Date: _____

Topic:
(Example)
•Weather

	Did you find what you needed?	
	Yes	No
1. _____		
2. _____		
3. _____		
4. _____		
5. _____		
6. _____		
7. _____		

Please provide any information that will help us offer the resources you need for your unit.

Student Curriculum Support Fill Rate

Please complete the information below, indicating the specific information you were searching for in the media center and whether you found that information. Thank You!

Number: _____

Date: _____

Topic:
(Example)
•Vietnam

	Did you find what you needed?	
	Yes	No
1. _____		
2. _____		
3. _____		
4. _____		
5. _____		
6. _____		
7. _____		

Please provide any information that will help us offer the resources you need for your assignment:

Independent Reading/Information Fill Rate

Please complete the information below, indicating the specific information you were searching for in the media center and whether you found that information. Thank You!

Number: _____

Date: _____

Topic, title, or activity:
   (Examples)
   • Horses
   • Just browsing
   • Playing chess

	Did you find what you needed?	
	Yes	No
1. _____		
2. _____		
3. _____		
4. _____		
5. _____		
6. _____		
7. _____		

Suggestions for other materials and activities here in the media center:

Collection Development Form

Subjects/Activities Not Found   Number of Times Sought

1. _____

2. _____

3. _____

4. _____

5. _____

6. _____

7. _____

8. _____

9. _____

10. _____

11. _____

12. _____

13. _____

14. _____

15. _____

16. _____

17. _____

18. _____

19. _____

20. _____

21. _____

22. _____

23. _____

24. _____

Online Resources Success Rate

The online resources success rate is a corollary to the electronic resources hit rate (a use measure described earlier). It is a calculation of the percentage of *successful* electronic information searches in relation to the number of overall searches conducted. Again, a great deal of money is being diverted to the technology. Is it justifying its existence? One of the best ways to determine this is a long-term study of successful searches, which must be tied to the curriculum support fill rate to be meaningful. Of course, collecting this statistic requires conversations with students and teachers as to the success (or lack thereof) of their searches — and a careful logging of that information.

How to Analyze and Use the Data

- When online resources are used to fulfill searches successfully on topics with no available resources within the school, they are justifying their monthly charges. And if similar searches are being performed over and over — and the information itself is not time sensitive — an additional piece of information is learned: the need for further in-center resources.

- Here again, combining this information with the furniture and equipment use rate can help justify additional computers with Internet access or Internet access networked to individual classrooms.

- Finally, look carefully at what the data are telling you. Perhaps the real information that you are getting is that further instruction on electronic searching, particularly Internet search strategies, may be all that is necessary to increase the percentages in this category.

The Measure at a Glance

Use the **online resources success rate** along with the electronic resources hit rate in assessing the online services in the media center. These data can be used to justify the money spent on electronic services, develop better training sessions and, with the furniture and equipment statistics, justify additional computers or networks.

After collecting your data, follow this pattern to calculate the measures that will support your case:

$$\text{Online Resources Success Rate} = \frac{\text{\# Successful Searches for Information or Material}}{\text{\# Searches}}$$

Chapter 3

Access Measures:
Media Specialist Availability Measures

Availability measures assess the essence of everything we do: Are we available to both teachers and students *when they need us*? Is our school library media center schedule so overloaded with permanently scheduled classes that we have no time to help those two third graders who want to find the name of the snake that they have caught? Are we so snowed under with classes that we cannot meet with the seventh-grade team as they plan their new unit on South Africa? Is our media center so busy with student CD-ROM and Internet searches that we can plan with our colleagues only "on the fly," before or after school? Is our schedule — either fixed or flexible — so heavily booked that we have resources stacked in the back room awaiting processing? All these scenarios indicate the need to begin gathering data to calculate the media specialist availability rate.

A subset of access measures, media specialist availability measures are strictly a school outcome measure and are based on the third role of the media specialist as defined in *Information Power*: the instructional consultant/collaborator. In other words, this subset is used to measure the media specialist's availability for meeting the teachers' and students' informational and instructional needs. Specifically, the data gathered are:

- the amount of time a media specialist is actually available to teach particular units of instruction

- the amount of time the media specialist actually spends planning with teachers for future instructional support

- the amount of time the media specialist consults with individual students and teachers about their research/information needs.

The reality is that these measures — planning opportunity measure, teaching availability measure, and the staff development opportunity measure — are interrelated and based upon similar data. Because of the similarities of the data, decide which measure will influence your principal and/or faculty most or will best sustain your argument for changing or augmenting your program. Initially, your point of presentation may be unclear, so just go ahead and begin collecting your data. It won't be long before you will be able to make a decision simply from the conversations and situations that arise as you survey.

Some suggestions:

- Generally speaking, one week in the fall and/or one week in the spring will *not* provide legitimate data for these measures. Start at the beginning of the school year or semester and collect forward.

The Measure at a Glance

Use the **media specialist availability** chart to examine how available you are to the teachers and students who need you. Use it to request more staff, budget increases, or schedule changes. All media specialist measures — planning opportunity rate, teaching availability rate, and staff development opportunity rate — are interrelated and based on similar data. To present a stronger case, use these three measures with other use and access measures.

Use the Sample Media Specialist Availability Charts on pages 41 – 42 as basic data collection forms. Adapt them to your needs.

Record all requests for the collection period and add up the total number of requests and the total filled or unfilled. Divide them into the categories you want to analyze.

For an example of how media specialist charts and measures can be used, read "The Case for Flexible Access," in which Mary uses a variety of availability measures, access measures, research, and the enticement of a pot of coffee to develop and successfully present her case for flexible scheduling.

At some point — usually at the end of a semester or after four to six months — you will find the data "speaking for itself." Only then should you put together your presentation. Having said this, I do believe that there may be times when a single week's data will support a case *provided* it is combined with other measures — such as the troubleshooting request rate. Just remember: more data make for better analysis.

• Make this process easy on yourself; you will have to live with it for a while. Keep a clipboard at your desk, on the circulation desk, around the teacher planning area or calendar so that you can jot down notes. Computerize this at the end of the day or week or, if you trust your memory *and* your clipboard, at the end of your survey time.

Figure 3-1

Sample Media Specialist Availability Chart

Date	Time	Teacher	Request	Response*
4/24	7:35	Smith	Send small groups of students to media center to research lives of first 5 presidents. Each group has diff. pres. Wants them to learn to use CD-ROM encyclop. then put into multimedia presentation.	Will teach whole class to use CD-ROM next week during scheduled period. Then small groups can come in while I teach classes. They're on their own. Can't do multimedia presentation skills with them because of time. They'll print out illustrations instead. (M)
	10:15	4th grade	Meet with them during planning time so we can plan weather unit.	Unable to because I am teaching Jones's 4th grade class — so she can plan! Arranged for *WeatherLinker* subscription. (U)
	12:05	Caitwell	Needed some books on butterflies — cocoon starting to split.	Helped her find books. Ate lunch at desk after she left since 12:30 class due. (F)
	1:35	Marlboro	Sent student to say network down.	Taught until 2:30. Fixed after school. (F)
	during day	12 students	Returning/checking out books without guidance	Teaching classes during their searches. (M)

* (F) filled;
 (M) modified, cannot be filled immediately;
 (U) unfilled, cannot be filled in a reasonable amount of time or legitimately does not satisfy either the teacher or specialist.

Develop your own shorthand. The sample form in Figure 3-1 is detailed for demonstration purposes. The blank form on page 41 is your form; abbreviate as time dictates — but *fill it out!* Your argument will be futile without records.

Notice that the sample chart (Figure 3-1) could provide data for either the teaching availability measure, the planning opportunity measure, or the staff development opportunity measure; it needs only to be interpreted for each. See Figure 3-2 for what a month's summary of the data might look like.

Secondary media specialists may find subject area calculations more effective than grade level calculations. For instance, if social studies or language arts teachers constantly request planning time or small group research time that you must modify, it may be time to calculate media specialist availability measures to justify additional staff.

Figure 3-2

Sample Media Specialist Availability Summary Chart

Requests	Week of 4/4 Modified/Unfilled (Total Requests)	Week of 4/11 Modified/Unfilled (Total Requests)	Week of 4/18 Modified/Unfilled (Total Requests)	Week of 4/25 Modified/Unfilled (Total Requests)
Planning with teams	1 (1)	0 (0)	3 (3)	1 (1)
Individual/ small group work	6 (8)	1 (3)	0 (6)	14 (17)
Whole class	0 (2)	1 (1)	2 (2)	1 (3)
Planning with individual teachers	8 (12)	12 (12)	8 (16)	11 (12)
Individual student request/search	73 (112)	65 (182)	93 (201)	34 (97)

Media Specialist Availability Chart

Date	Time	Teacher	Request	Response*

* (F) filled;
  (M) modified, cannot be filled immediately;
  (U) unfilled, cannot be filled in a reasonable amount of time or legitimately does not satisfy either the
      teacher or specialist.

Media Specialist Availability Summary

Requests	Week of _____ Modified/Unfilled (Total Requests)	Week of _____ Modified/Unfilled (Total Requests)	Week of _____ Modified/Unfilled (Total Requests)	Week of _____ Modified/Unfilled (Total Requests)

Planning Opportunity Rate

The planning opportunity rate is the percentage of times a media specialist is able to completely fill a teacher's or team's request for assistance in planning a lesson or unit of instruction. If you want to present a need for more planning time with teachers, you would pull out the two planning categories to calculate your planning opportunity rate and would indicate that you were unable to *completely* fulfill any team planning requests for the month of April, or there was a 0 percent grade level planning opportunity rate for that month (see Figure 3-2). Notice the italicized word, *completely*. In your notes, you have detailed information about each request. For instance, although your presence would have facilitated the fourth-grade teachers' April 24 planning meeting when they discussed implementing the telecommunications program *WeatherLinker*, you did at least set it up for them — a modified request.

Frankly, some arbitrary decisions may be necessary as you calculate planning opportunity rates. If you are teaching classes so that teachers can plan together or individually, it will be impossible for you

The Measure at a Glance

Use the **planning opportunity rate** to request more planning time with teachers, a more flexible schedule, and more staff. Use in combination with use measures and materials availability rates to augment your documentation.

Use the Sample Media Specialist Availability Chart (Figure 3.1) on page 39 as a model for collecting data, and then follow this pattern to calculate the measures that will support your case:

$$\text{Planning opportunity rate} = 100\% - \frac{\text{\# modified or unfilled planning requests}}{\text{\# planning requests received from teachers}}$$

For an example of how to use this measure, read "The Case for Flexible Access," in which Mary uses the planning opportunity rate as part of her argument for flexible scheduling.

to be present at planning meetings. If, however, individuals or groups come to you to request unit materials or activities — or schedule additional planning time before or after school or during your lunch because you are teaching during their planning times — you can log this as a modified or unfilled planning request. Decide at the outset how you will log these requests, being mindful of the political implications of each choice.

How to Analyze and Use the Data

- Here is the perfect opportunity to draw upon your use measures and materials availability measures to present an effective case for schedule modification or staff increase. Looking at planning requests and comparing them with data from circulation rates, turnover rates, curriculum support fill rates, and independent reading/information support fill rate offers potentially interesting and compelling information. For instance, low curriculum support fill rates coupled with a 55 percent planning opportunity rate suggests that teachers would benefit from more assistance from the media specialist in choosing resources for classroom units. Were the circulation rate or electronic resource hit rate also low, a case could be made that expensive resources were being wasted because teachers and the media specialist did not have adequate time to plan for and implement their use. A more flexible schedule might open up opportunities for doing so.

- Either professional or clerical staff could be justified in certain situations where planning requests were high and opportunity low. In schools in which permanently scheduled classes are required, can two professionals share teaching responsibilities, thus freeing someone to meet planning needs most of the time? Or can an assistant be responsible for story time or fixed check-out times in order to open up planning opportunities for the professional?

Hot Spots!

- Presenting this type of information can be tricky. At no time should we give the impression that we are not trying our hardest to fulfill teacher and student requests. Therefore, it is mandatory that we preface every discussion with the statement (and the evidence) that everything has been done to meet teacher and student needs. We must emphasize that the presentation is being made in a good faith attempt to give better, more efficient service to teachers and students throughout the school year.

- Some administrators (and fellow teachers) will see nothing wrong with planning on the fly or, worse yet, forsaking your lunch period to help a teacher find butterfly books! Situations like this may require, in addition to extraordinary tact and patience, specific reference to other media specialists' schedules in your district or state, the research on flexible scheduling, or even reference to state regulations regarding the teaching day, if you are fortunate enough to fall under those guidelines.

Teaching Availability Rate

Your teaching availability rate is the percentage of time that you are available to work with individuals, small groups, or whole classes at the specific request of a teacher. It is calculated from the same data as the planning opportunity measure, this time using individual/small group work and whole class work categories. Those data are *in addition* to your daily fixed schedule of whole-class instruction blocks to which you are already assigned. You are looking for requests you either can't fulfill or must modify in order to support. Thus, in April your teaching availability rate was 40 percent — or 38 percent for small group instruction (21 unfilled/modified requests out of 34) and 50 percent for whole-class instruction (4 unfilled/modified out of 8 requests) (see Sample Availability chart on pages 39 – 40). In other words, you were available to work with classes specifically, without modifica-

*The Measure
        at a Glance*

Use the **teaching availability rate** to justify a more flexible schedule and additional staff. Other measures to use in conjunction with the teaching availability rate are the in-library use rates, the electronic resource hit rates, and the online resources success rates.

Refocus the data that you collected for planning availability rates using the sample charts on pages 41 – 42, and then follow this pattern to calculate the measures that will support your case:

$$\text{Teaching availability rate} = 100\% - \frac{\text{\# modified or unfilled teaching requests}}{\text{\# teaching requests received from teachers}}$$

For an example of how these measures can be used, read "The Case for Flexible Access," in which Mary uses the teaching availability rate as one of the measures to justify her need for flexible scheduling.

tion, at a teacher's request, a total of 17 out of 42 times, or 40 percent of the time, for a teaching availability rate of 40 percent.

Likewise, if you maintain open circulation while you are teaching classes, thus allowing students to check in and out resources without your — or an assistant's — guidance, you potentially have unfilled or modified student requests or searches. Therefore, if during the month of April you could assist only 327 of the 592 students who individually came into the media center, your media specialist availability rate for working with students was 55 percent during April.

$$592 \text{ students}$$
$$- \ 265 \text{ student requests unfilled/modified}$$
$$= \ 327 \text{ students helped}$$

327 divided by 592 = 45%

100 minus 45 = 55%

How to Analyze and Use the Data

- Just as planning opportunity measures, in combination with a variety of materials use measures, can help justify a more flexible schedule as well as additional staff, teaching availability measures can support the same requests. Simply refocus your arguments from planning categories and data to the teaching categories and data.

- This is a particularly opportune time to pull in your in-library use rates and electronic resource hit rates, as well as the online resources success rates. The more often you are available to teach *relevant* use of materials, the better these statistics ought to become. Thus, although initially low materials use rates and teaching availability rates can be used to justify scheduling changes and additional personnel, documentation of gradual improvement can prove that the changes and additions are effective.

Hot Spots!

- For elementary or middle-school media specialists, this calculation has the potential to be loaded with land mines. In actuality, you will be asking to teach what your teachers are requesting rather than what you are already teaching. While media specialists know that this is not an either/or situation, don't assume that administrators will. Teacher support will be vital here. Testimonies asserting the importance of blocks of time for research and activities will go a long way in helping you make your case for a more flexible schedule.

- Even though teacher availability data may be easier to gather and garner actual support for, it ultimately may not be as critical to the health of your media program — and your whole school's academic success — as the planning opportunity measures. Most teachers cannot envision the subtle rewards that planning time with a media specialist can provide, so you may have to structure your justification within a teaching availability framework. This is certainly acceptable, since the means will justify the ends, but be aware that the planning time accrued from this argument will be critical, so don't sabotage yourself at the beginning of the change process.

Troubleshooting Request Rate

The troubleshooting request rate calculates any request for assistance in solving an equipment problem. How many times must you stop working with students to re-boot the circulation program or troubleshoot a balky file server? How often are you asked to leave the media center to figure out why the VCR won't play or the classroom computer won't access the network? In these days, when equipment maintenance can overwhelm any school library media specialist and completely usurp any sort of curriculum and program support, calculating the troubleshooting request rate may help you get some technical assistance. Logging the number of requests, the amount of time each requires, and the possible consequence of this time commitment will give you and others an idea of the possible loss of instructional support time for students and teachers.

Figure 3-3

Sample Troubleshooting Request Log

	Request	Time	Within Media Center	Outside Media Center	Instruction Interrupted*
Before School	Load HyperStudio on Ms. Charles's computer	5 minutes		✔	
	Get VCR working in Mr. Smith's room	20 minutes		✔	
1st Period	Network down	1 ½ hours	✔		✔

* Media specialist instructional time.

How to Analyze and Use the Data

- Determining the troubleshooting request rate can provide a compelling statement of how technology is impacting your overall media program as well as your own job description (see Figure 3-3). Have you become a technician rather than a vital part of your school's instructional program? Does your job description, as well as your evaluation criteria, accurately reflect the skills that you have had to learn over the past several years? Calculating this measure by itself can help you document information that you already know to be the case.

- If the real issue is not just one of validating additional responsibilities but also of asserting the need for additional staffing so you can return to curriculum support duties, pair the troubleshooting request rate with the curriculum support request rate (page 26) to document teacher and student needs while validating the role that technology is playing throughout the whole instructional program. Likewise adding other media specialist availability measures provides additional information to justify a staffing increase and/or a change from a fixed to a flexible schedule.

Hot Spots! Beware the faculty or administration that will not see beyond the technology and its upkeep. If you have any doubts about whether they will be able to understand that you really have taken on what eventually will become two full-time positions — school library media specialist *and* technology specialist — or if you suspect that they would be perfectly satisfied with your role only as technology troubleshooter, make sure you calculate other measures such as curriculum support request rate and media specialist availability as well. Do not present the troubleshooting rate by itself under these circumstances!

The Measure
at a Glance

Use **troubleshooting request rates** to request more staff or schedule changes.

Figure 3-3, Sample Troubleshooting Request Log on page 47, shows how to collect data for the troubleshooting request rate. Then follow these patterns to calculate the measures that will support your case:

$$\text{Average \# requests daily} = \frac{\text{Total \# requests per week}}{\text{5 days per week}}$$

$$\text{Average \# hours troubleshooting per day} = \frac{\text{Total time spent troubleshooting}}{\text{\# days}}$$

$$\text{\% troubleshooting requiring leaving media center} = \frac{\text{\# requests requiring leaving center}}{\text{Total \# troubleshooting requests}}$$

$$\text{\% troubleshooting interrupting instruction} = \frac{\text{\# requests that interrupted instructional time}}{\text{Total \# troubleshooting requests}}$$

For an example of how these measures can be used, read "The Case for a Technology Assistant," in which Paul uses his troubleshooting request rate to support his request for a technical assistant.

Staff Development Opportunity Rate

The staff development opportunity rate is a calculation of the number and kind of staff development opportunities available to an educational community. Calculating them may not produce additional staff or free up a fixed schedule, but it will allow you to begin to document the effectiveness of staff development in the use of resources. In education's current quest to prove that technology is making a difference in the teaching/learning process, figuring the staff development opportunity rates — and the subsequent differences that both the technology and the staff development are making — may enhance the job security and reputations of many of us. These calculations also may help us save those other resources — books and AV — that are being threatened as schools across the country jump on the technology bandwagon.

Interestingly enough, these very important statistics are some of the easiest to calculate. For the staff development opportunity rate, simply figure the number of courses offered during a school year. The teacher attendance rate merely involves the percentage of teachers availing themselves of these opportunities at a given workshop or throughout the year. Interesting spins can be put on the data: the number of workshops offered that directly meet the schoolwide goal of integrating technology into the curriculum, for instance; or the percentage of staff who attend staff development opportunities when continuing education units are offered as opposed to those where they are not.

The best information for our own use, however, will come from analyzing the materials use rates after staff development has been offered to see what types of staff development work best for our particular faculty and how much is needed before teaching behaviors begin to change. We may even begin to learn when the best time for staff development is for our particular faculty. Teachers may be telling us that they prefer workshops on teacher workdays, but their actual attendance may point to after school or the summer months. The ability to refer to this data when

Hot Spots!

- Sometimes teachers are not ready for staff development even if the principal, central office, or School Improvement Team tells them that they are. If this is the case, you probably will find little difference in resources use — or perhaps even *less* use. If your statistics indicate this phenomenon, you may need to offer the same or similar opportunities at a later date.

- One-on-one staff development or tutorial staff development at time of need may be the best form of training that you can offer your individual faculty members, but significant results may be difficult to report to your principal. The example of the art teacher (pages 53 – 54) is an obvious one, as would be the electronic resources hit rate after teaching social studies teachers how to use the *Thomas* Internet site or the *Time Almanac*. While you may realize the difference in collection use after you booktalked all the special Vietnam War resources, use figures might be too subtle for anyone other than fellow media specialists to appreciate. Savor these little victories and tout the more obvious ones.

- The time commitment necessary in planning staff development opportunities may be overlooked by teachers and administrators alike. Few people are going to be cognizant of the amount of time it takes to develop individual tutorials for new CD-ROMs or the number of evening hours of reading and preparation required to booktalk those Vietnam resources. Hopefully, the increased use of the collection and the more effective, efficient use of the technology will begin to be apparent to all teachers and administrators, and your statistics will help them make the connection between the two. As this happens, flexible schedules and additional personnel will become obvious, and hopefully not fiscally unattainable, consequences.

- Finally, taking on the staff development responsibilities for a school may be tricky. Principals and staff — and sometimes even the central office — must give us "permission" to perform this role. The reality is that we may have to go slowly, especially if we're newly employed, planning one-on-one opportunities for individual teachers and making subtle, tactful suggestions for larger, more global staff development opportunities.

making scheduling and topic decisions can lessen criticism and foster good decision making.

A caveat is in order here: At best, a media specialist can be responsible only for the staff development within his or her individual building. Systemwide staff development, though often requested and organized by building-level staff, is the responsibility of central office personnel unless otherwise designated. This does not preclude us from using the data, however, nor does it keep us from making suggestions based on our observations.

How do you calculate staff development opportunity rates? First, consider what you actually want to know or prove. Are your teachers requesting more staff development than your principal or central office staff is willing to schedule? If that's the case, then calculate the staff development opportunity rate. You can be as general or specific as you need. For instance, your chart may look like this:

Figure 3-4

Sample Staff Development Request Rate Chart

	Requests Made	Staff Development Offered	% Filled
January	18	2	11%
February	12	2	16%
March	4	3	75%
April	10	0	0%
May	0	0	0%

Obvious holes exist in this data. Is the staff development offered actually meeting the requests being made? There is no way to tell, even though it would *appear* that someone responded to the January/February requests in March. The lack of staff development in April may be linked directly to Spring vacations. Inadequate as they may be, these data at least imply a great deal and offer ammunition for more staff development.

Or perhaps the administration or central office is very staff development oriented, yet the staff development they offer does not seem to be meeting the needs of your faculty. You can assemble your data as done in Figure 3-5. The key to reporting these data are honesty and reality. One cannot expect immediate gratification as far as staff development is concerned unless a person is simply lucky. Good staff development takes time to prepare. The key to accurate statistics is to see if, over a period of several months, staff development needs are being met.

What happens if your teachers are requesting certain staff development but then don't avail themselves of the opportunity once it is offered? What if the School Improvement Team targets the integration of telecommunications into the curriculum as a schoolwide goal, sets up the staff development to support it, and wants to know if the teachers are participating? Your data might take the form of Figure 3-6.

Figure 3-5

Sample Staff Development Data Chart

	Requests Made (topic and number)	Staff Development Offered by School (or district office)	Unmet Needs of Previous Months	Current Unmet Needs
January	• Spreadsheets (3) • Telecomputing (5) • How to use the new CD-ROMs in media center (10) • Desktop Publishing (1)	• Learning to use Word 6.1 • Installing Windows 95 • Self-guided tutorial in media center of *Time Almanac *Encarta *A.D.A.M.	N/A	9 of 19 or 47%
February	• Spreadsheets (3) • Telecomputing (8) • Identifying weather resources (4) • Grade programs (22) • Desktop Publishing (3)	• Beginner's Excel • Using *WeatherLinker* with your class • Using a camcorder to enhance student research projects	1 of 19 or 6%	26 of 40 or 65%

Figure 3-6

Sample Staff Development Tracking Form

Courses Requested/ Scheduled for 1st Semester	Attendance*	%
Introduction to Telecommunications (Districtwide course)		
• Overview (9/18, 3:30 – 5:00)	33	100%
• How to set up equipment (9/25, 3:30 – 5:00)	25	75%
• Choosing a telecomputing activity (10/2, 3:30 – 5:00)	25	75%
Using National Geographic KidsNet programs (workshop consultants here for all-day workshop 11/7, 8:00 – 3:00)	10	30%
Integrating writing assignments with telecommunications (teacher workday 11/11, 9:00 – 12)	20	66%
Math activities with telecommunications (12/6, 3:30 – 5)	3	9%
* 33 possible attendees		

Staff Development Data Chart

Month	Requests Made (topic and number)	Staff Development Offered by school (or district office)	Unmet Needs of Previous Months	Current Unmet Needs

How To Analyze and Use the Data

Interesting data! Several possibilities are suggested as we study these statistics:

- Everyone started out participating in the telecommunications series, but eight appeared to drop out immediately — for whatever reason.

- Only ten people participated in the day-long workshop in spite of the fact that national consultants had been hired to train teachers on a commercial program. Were substitute teachers the problem, or had many already planned to use other activities or resources?

- The teacher workday attracted a good following, but the December program did not. Was this a scheduling phenomenon (holiday deadlines?) or were more people interested in using telecommunications to teach English than Math?

- Would attendance have been better if CEU credit had been offered?

- All in all, this appears to have been a fairly successful staff development series. Is it because it was a schoolwide goal, or because it was organized for incremental skill building rather than a one-shot fix — or both?

You can probably think of other variations for collecting this information, but its usefulness is unlimited.

Even more fascinating, however, is combining the analysis of these staff development opportunity statistics with materials use rates. Once teachers have availed themselves of staff development opportunities, does their use of the actual resources improve? As media specialists, we would certainly hope and assume so, but statistics will either confirm or deny the hypothesis.

What use measures can be paired with staff development opportunity measures? Practically all of them. The key, however, is to make sure that you have logged your baseline data before you begin. The questions to ask are: Are certain specific resources (e.g., the CD-ROM encyclopedias), areas of the collection (e.g., 520s [weather] or 949s [Vietnam War]), or equipment (e.g., video camera) more heavily and effectively used after those staff development opportunities? A good example might be a media-center use measures. Are teachers using the media center more after certain staff development opportunities? Do the teachers who have participated in these opportunities use the media center more often and more effectively after targeted staff development? For instance, let's say you have had a difficult time getting the art teacher to use the media center and its resources. After you schedule times during her planning period to demonstrate the *Louvre* videodisc, the *Vatican* Internet site, and the numerous art books in the print collection, she brings her students into the media center to explore topics for projects dealing with Renaissance art. Your media center use rate statistics increase substantially in the area of eighth-grade art appreciation class use.

Or look at circulation of materials using the same example. Both the art teacher and her students may begin to check out art books. Where the 700s had previously logged only marginal use, they now have revitalized circulation.

Figure 3-7

Sample Staff Development/Circulation Rates

1997 – 98   700s circulation rate:

               53 books   47/student circs
                           6/teacher circs

Art teacher staff development conducted week of September 25 during planning period

1998
(Sept. – Dec.)   700s circulation rate:

               157 books   122/student circs
                        35/teacher circs

Materials use rate increase: 150%
(directly related to in-house, one-on-one staff development)

Similar calculations can be developed for in-library use rates, electronic resources hit rates, and turnover rates — even with furniture and equipment use rates. For instance, going back to the staff development workshop "Using video cameras to enhance student research projects," your log might have an entry similar to this one:

Figure 3-8

Sample Video Camera Use Data

Video camera checkouts
     September – December: 16 times/3 teachers

Workshops offered:
     Using video cameras to enhance student research projects (3 sessions)
          January 14, January 21, January 29
     Attendance: 16 teachers completed all 3 sessions

Video camera checkouts
     February – May: 53 times/10 teachers

Equipment use rate increase: 165%
     (directly related to in-house staff development)

In order to expand the usefulness of previous measures discussions, the second half of the book will look at specific case studies that apply the measures themselves to authentic, school library media center situations.

The Measure
at a Glance

Use the **staff development opportunity rate** to document the effectiveness of staff development in the use of resources, to demonstrate the differences that both technology and staff development are making, and to save resources that are threatened because sometimes schools focus almost solely on technology.

Use the Sample Staff Development Data Chart and the Sample Staff Development Tracking Form on pages 51 – 52 to organize your data collection, and then follow this pattern to calculate the measures that will support your case:

$$\text{Staff development request rate} = 100\% - \frac{\text{\# unmet requests for staff development}}{\text{\# staff development requests received from administrators and teachers}}$$

$$\text{Staff development attendance rate} = \frac{\text{\# staff attending sessions}}{\text{\# enrolled staff}}$$

Part II

Output Measures in Action

Chapter 4

The Case for Flexible Access

Mary was frustrated. Every hour of every day at her elementary school was filled. Darling cherubs filed in and out in carefully orchestrated lines to sit at tables, listen to a story or absorb the library skill of the day, spend twenty minutes checking out their weekly books, and then returning to class. Only lunch held any spontaneity, for then she might connect with a teacher or student and help them find what they really needed to teach a lesson or complete an assignment. And if this happened, she began the afternoon hungry.

Determined to get her teachers and principal to see the logic in freeing up her schedule to work with teachers and students, Mary began to plan. What measures would make the best case for flexible access? The media center use rate was a logical choice; so was the curriculum support request rate. The curriculum support fill rate might be a tactic, too. But the heart of the matter was the media specialist availability measures. Media specialist availability, planning opportunity, and teaching availability comprised the essentials of the case she wished to build. After reviewing the data-gathering steps that each required, she finally settled upon all three of the availability measures and the curriculum support fill rate as the most logical ones to pursue.

But Mary soon realized her problem was larger than simply collecting data and reporting it in a logical manner. Her teachers had no idea how a flexible schedule might benefit them personally; everyone in the school seemed content with the status quo. Yes, occasionally a teacher might drift into the media center with a plan for her students to do some research, but Mary had little trouble integrating it into the weekly library skills lesson. Her greatest challenge would be to create enough awareness of what was missing in her program to cause her teachers to desire a change in the first place!

That weekend Mary devised a strategy. Frustrated as she was, she realized that this was no short-term project. The actual calculations of the measures had to be put on hold for at least a few months while she laid the groundwork for her case.

Monday morning dawned rainy and cold, a perfect excuse to hit the snooze button, but Mary was not to be deterred. Grabbing the extra coffee pot that had been in the cupboard since her wedding, she headed for school early. After brewing and pouring herself a cup, she started for Donna's room. Donna was probably the best teacher in the school. Creative, energetic, and bright, she always had new ideas for her fifth graders. Mary approached her tentatively — after all, it *was* Monday morning. "Didn't I hear you mention that you were beginning your unit on Canada this week?" she asked.

"Yes," Donna replied with a smile. "I'm going to introduce the Provinces to the class today."

"Well, I was just thinking it might be fun to let your kids have an opportunity to use the CD-ROM encyclopedias to find out some information about Canada — and we just received the new set of *Lands and Peoples*. If you have a few minutes this afternoon or during your planning period, perhaps we could talk about it. Oh, and by the way, there's a pot of coffee in my office. Come get a cup before the kids arrive."

Next she headed for the teachers' lounge where a few sleepyheads were just checking in. Inviting everyone she met to bring a mug and follow their noses, she hurried back to her office to get ready for her nine o'clock class.

Over the next several months, Mary was a dervish of activity. She and Donna designed a research project centered on the Canadian Provinces. The class was divided into groups according to specific provinces, and each group received individual search instructions during their scheduled library time while the others were exploring books and other media center resources dealing with their geographical areas. After two regularly scheduled class periods, one group remained to be taught, so Mary volunteered to have them return during her lunch so that they would not be too far behind the others. After all, it would be another week before she saw them again!

Donna's class was not the only one receiving special attention. Mary approached the kindergarten and first-grade teachers about allowing their children to check out and return books daily during the thirty minutes before her first class. Since their focus was reading immersion, they jumped at the chance — and did not hesitate to tell the other teachers how excited their children were to be able to visit the media center whenever they finished their books rather than having to wait until library time. Soon the upper grades were clamoring for early morning checkout, too — a request Mary was delighted to fill.

The coffee pot became a magnet for conversation. Mary often shared a cup with teachers and listened as they discussed their plans for the day or week. Occasionally, she would make a suggestion for an activity that she could do during library time that would support a teaching unit. Other times she would slip away from the conversation and return a few minutes later with a book or video that fit right in. Gradually, some of the teachers began to seek her advice as they waited for a new pot to perk, and occasionally one or two would drop off a pound of coffee or a plate of goodies to share.

A milestone was reached the morning Donna scurried in for a quick cup. Never one to waste a second, she immediately began an informal evaluation of her Province Project with Mary as she stirred in extra sugar and creamer.

"It was wonderful!" she told the other two teachers waiting their turn. "The kids learned so much and enjoyed it immensely. The only problem was having enough time. It took two weeks of library time to get everyone using the CD-ROMs, and even then Mary had to give up her lunch to train the last group. If only we had had a couple of hours in the media center on that first day to get everyone up to speed at the same time. This just doesn't make sense!"

"TA DAH!" Mary rejoiced to herself as Donna hurried off. "It will soon be time to make my move."

Little did she know. That afternoon Sherry dropped by the media center. "Donna and I were talking while the children were at PE," she said. "I'm interested in having my students do a unit like her Province Project — you know, with library time and all. She volunteered to let me have her next week's time — it comes right after mine — so that everyone can get CD-ROM instruction on the same day. I'll just return the favor the next time she needs double time in the media center."

These were conversations and opportunities not to be missed. Time to begin to gather availability statistics!

That afternoon Mary dropped by the store on the way home, picking up a couple of clipboards especially for her data. She had decided that the informal approach was best for her: just a daily fill-in-the-blanks from the forms photocopied from this book. "I know myself well enough to realize that my plan has to be scribbling only enough to jog my memory as people go in and out. I'm going to have to vow not to leave school every afternoon until I've filled in completely all those cryptic request notes that I've jotted down throughout the day. I'll lose my credibility if I don't!"

Mary was amazed at how many entries could be tallied at the end of the day as F, M, or U. And sometimes this designation was the hardest part of the record keeping!

The next day the clipboard and form were readily available as Mary went about her day. Each request was briefly alluded to in journal format, beginning with Donna and Sherry's time swap. Mary was amazed at how many entries could be tallied at the end of the day as F, M, or U. And sometimes this designation was the hardest part of the record keeping! If she had to postpone helping a teacher or troubleshooting an equipment failure, did she consider this a modified or a filled request? After all, she ultimately filled that request, but within a different time frame than desired.

After several days of indecision, Mary finally decided that consistency really was the most important aspect of this record keeping. Therefore, she logged as filled (F) any request that ultimately was completed to everyone's satisfaction during that particular school day. Requests that had to be carried over to another day, or requests that satisfied the teacher or student but really flew in the face of good librarianship garnered an (M) designation.

The next weekend, Mary took her records home and tallied the results. The first data set was an eye-opener:

Figure 4-1

Sample Tally of Requests Modified or Unfilled

Types of Requests	Modified or Unfilled (Total)
Planning with teams	0 (0)
Individual/small groups	7 (14)
Whole class	0 (8)
Planning with individual teachers	4 (18)
Individual students	89 (144)

First, she suspected that she would never log anything but zeros in the planning with teams column. That request would never even occur to her teachers, because it had never been an option. She taught their students to free them up for that planning time. Here would be the major stumbling block to flexible access, and logging that request as a U, M, or F would not take place anytime soon!

Second, she really could fill the whole-class requests most of the time. Only when a teacher needed more than her weekly fifty-minute block would it ever even be an issue. But here was the big surprise: it was the students who appeared to have their requests most often modified or unfilled! Somehow she could manage an acceptable response to a teacher's needs. Students, on the other hand, moved in and out of the media center constantly, like so many waves on the beach. If she didn't catch them at the moment, far too many were gone, on to another assignment, back to class with a not-quite-acceptable new book, not getting exactly the information needed to answer their question or write their report.

As she contemplated this surprising piece of information, she suddenly realized that this might be the best argument for flexible access after all — the students! In a school of conscientious, student-centered teachers, what better justification for any change than that it was the best way to educate students. Yes, she would indeed focus on planning with teachers and small-group instruction, but her case would hinge on how all of this affected student opportunities in the media center.

Now that she had determined the focus of her argument, the data keeping for the next six weeks was an easier task psychologically. The fourth week into the study, she took another leap. She decided to calculate the curriculum support fill rate for both teachers and students just as she had planned, but she added the independent reading/information fill rate to the data set, too. If she were going to focus on student access as justification for flexible scheduling, she reasoned, she needed this final piece of the puzzle.

Flipping through the book, she found the forms she needed, but was pulled up short when she realized that the independent reading/information fill rate and the curriculum support fill rate were designed for middle- and high-school students. She immediately understood why. How on earth could a primary student complete these forms without adult assistance? And *any* elementary student would find it impossible to decide what form to use. After recovering from her initial dismay, she made a decision: only the fifth graders would complete a questionnaire, and she would combine the curriculum support fill rate form and the independent reading/information fill rate form into one student information form. She'd talk to their teachers the next day.

The next afternoon Mary made a point of touching base with each fifth-grade teacher to explain her idea. In their next library time, she would introduce the concept of surveying to compile information and show students a copy of the actual form. Then she would request that they complete one form each as they selected their book for the week. Thereafter, they would complete a form each time they came into the media center in search of a book or other information. Since she met all fifth-grade classes on Wednesday, the survey time frame would run through the next Friday — eight days of data.

As luck would have it, Mary also was able to introduce the curriculum support fill rate forms to her colleagues at the Wednesday afternoon faculty meeting, so both the student and the teacher data covered approximately the same eight-day period. While the fifth graders responded to her lesson and assignment with an immediate "Cool!" her colleagues were skeptical. In spite of her assurances that the entire process was for only eight days — and she certainly didn't expect them to fill out a survey if they were rushed — she left the faculty meeting discouraged.

The next morning, however, again around the coffee pot, she had a second chance. Explaining to two or three friends as they sipped coffee that this short survey would help her determine gaps in the collection and services she needed to provide was less intimidating than an entire faculty in a formal setting. And the teachers were more receptive, too. Perhaps it was the sun streaming through the windows, the fact that it was Thursday — who knows? By the time school officially began that day, Mary believed several teachers would fill out surveys as they moved in and out of the media center.

Over the next seven days, most of them did complete surveys. Often, Mary would pick up one of the five clipboards she had designated "teacher" clipboards, approach the teacher as she searched for materials, suggest several options, and then quietly move about her tasks. Other times she would simply gesture to the pile of clipboards as she continued working with students.

The fifth graders needed no reminder. Proud to be given this responsibility, they picked up their forms as they explored the collection before and after school as well as during the day when she was working with other classes.

As she glanced at the completed forms throughout the survey period, she knew she was on the right track. Thank goodness most everyone had included the time and date! These two pieces of information allowed her to track exactly what she was doing while both teachers and students were searching for resources. As you would expect, the teachers did a better job of finding materials on their own, but even they alluded to frustration at not finding items in the comment section of their forms. One teacher complained, "Why can't everything be shelved in one area? I don't have time to run all over this library!" and another left her a note, "I'll be back at 3. I need help finding this information."

The children's comments were sometimes poignant. One child — she knew it was James — lamented, "I don't know the books like Mrs. Carter does" and another listed "Mrs. Lutz's assignment" in the topic line and checked "No" under "Did you find what you need?" Those children needed help, she thought indignantly!

The weekend after the survey time frame was completed, Mary willingly sent her husband off to play golf. After looking at the surveys and reading all the comments, she decided that her best approach would be a comparison chart: the curriculum support fill rate during the times she was available to assist teachers and students compared to the curriculum support fill rate when she was unavailable. She separated both sets of forms into two piles, one for times when she was available to help, the other for when she was not. She then tallied them exactly as the book suggested, making note to return to the forms before she compiled her next book order.

When she finished, Mary had to admit that even though the data proved her point, it wasn't as dramatic as she had hoped. Her teacher curriculum support fill rate was 93 percent when she was available, 87 percent when she wasn't; the student curriculum support fill rate was 98 percent when she was, 79 percent when she was not. Again, the student data were the most compelling, just as she had planned, but her other data would have to be more convincing if she were going to persuade everyone that change was necessary. But that was what all this work was for, right? It was time to compile all the data and make her case.

She had six weeks of planning request data, as well as the comparison with the curriculum support fill rate for when she was available to help and when she was not. Since she had been conscientious in logging all requests as they came in and analyzing them each weekend, the summary data took only minutes to compile. It looked like this:

Figure 4-2

Six-Week Total of Requests Modified or Unfilled

	Week of 2/11 M/U(T)*	Week of 2/18 M/U(T)	Week of 2/25 M/U(T)	Week of 3/4 M/U(T)	Week of 3/11 M/U(T)	Week of 3/18 M/U(T)	Total	% M/U
Planning with teams	0 (0)	0 (0)	0 (0)	0 (0)	0 (0)	0 (0)	0 (0)	0 (0)
Individual/ small groups	14 (17)	12 (15)	14 (18)	9 (14)	6 (12)	12 (14)	67 (90)	74%
Whole class	0 (8)	0 (11)	1 (11)	0 (7)	0 (5)	0 (0)	1 (42)	2%
Planning w/ individual teachers	4 (18)	7 (16)	3 (10)	6 (15)	5 (13)	5 (12)	30 (84)	36%
Individual students	89 (144)	93 (159)	81 (130)	102 (172)	97 (159)	76 (134)	538 (898)	60%

* M/U = Modified/Unfilled; T = Total

Just as she had expected, the impact of a fixed schedule, while important in her work with teachers, was greatest with the children. Sixty percent of student requests had to be modified or go completely unfilled. Significantly, 74 percent of the individual/small group requests from teachers were either modified or unfilled. The ultimate impact here was on students as well. The data spoke clearly.

But how best to present it, she wondered. The principal needed to know and her media advisory committee (MAC) did, too. The MAC was a group of grade-level representatives who gave her input on classroom needs and helped her make the hard purchasing decisions. Often they were her strongest advocates when she had to make a difficult decision. Just last fall they had come to her defense when she had decided to upgrade the circulation system with the PTA money rather than buy a single classroom a new computer and printer. They had helped her make that call, and they were vocal in their belief that this decision was the best for the entire school. If she could convince them of the need for flexible scheduling, she was home free!

Whom to talk with first was her next decision. Actually, if the principal was planning to attend the next MAC meeting, she could make one convincing argument. Mr. Taylor often wandered in the media center just to visit with children and see what was going on, so the next day, Mary approached him. Unless, an emergency came up, he planned to attend next Monday's meeting. Mary was delighted.

As the week passed, Mary became uneasy. Perhaps she should talk with Mr. Taylor before the MAC meeting. Her opportunity came Thursday afternoon as she was checking out of school. Mr. Taylor was leaning back in his office chair; no one else was around.

"Mind if I talk to you a minute?" she inquired.

"Sure thing, Mary, come in."

"I won't stay long, but I just wanted to share with you an idea I'll present at the MAC on Monday."

"Okay, shoot!"

"I'm going to make a case for adding flexibility to the library schedule. The more I've talked with teachers and students — the more I've watched them — the more concerned I have become. Teachers need blocks of time in the media center so that their students have enough time to do some real, in-depth exploration into a subject. They need to be able to make an assignment and not be forced to wait three or four weeks before their children have even had a chance to learn how to use the newest CD-ROM. They need enough time for their assignment to have some continuity.

"And the children, so often they simply need me. They need for me to be available to help them find resources that will allow them to complete an assignment, or find a book to read, or to learn what insect they found on the playground. Yesterday my heart just broke. Here I was teaching Ms. Griffin's class when five fifth graders from Ms. Donovan's class appeared. They had begun to talk about the Canadian form of government, and they wanted to find out how their Parliament differed from our Congress. Well, they went over to the encyclopedias, picked up the P volume, and headed back to class. The reason I know this is because Donovan came to the media center after school — with the P volume. She expressed frustration that this was all the information we had on the Canadian Parliament. When I assured her that we certainly had much more information than that P volume, she wondered aloud why her students returned to class with so little. I explained that I had been involved with Griffin's class, but that we could certainly find lots of materials about the Canadian government if I had about thirty to forty-five minutes with her students today. Of course, the only time we could find that I wasn't teaching other classes was today's lunch hour — so they came then."

"You didn't get lunch, Mary?"

"Well, I ate a cup of yogurt between Donovan's kids and Marshall's class. Anyway, during lunch we checked the catalog and found six different books on Canada that talked about their government; we even found a video about Canada. Tommy, bless him, started flipping through the books and announced that he didn't see any chart that would allow him to compare the U.S. and Canada, so we started looking in the CD-ROM encyclopedia to find a chart of the United States government so we could compare the two. Well, obviously they didn't come close to finishing, but they'll be back tomorrow — and I found the Canadian Parliament's Web site on the Internet this afternoon and ..."

"Mary, what's the problem? Are you hungry?" her principal interrupted.

"Come on, Mr. Taylor. You know that isn't the point. We need a way to free up my schedule so that I can truly meet the needs of both the teachers and students in this school."

"Well, I would argue that you *are* meeting those needs by providing planning time for the teachers, Mary."

"That certainly is one way, sir. But I would argue that that isn't the best, most educationally sound way. I would argue that having a schedule that encourages teachers to sign up for blocks of time so that their questions — and the answers to those questions — can become meaningful learning opportunities rather than superficial blips on the school-day screen would be truly meeting the needs of teachers. And even more important, helping students understand how to pose questions and retrieve information to provide answers — real answers to real questions — is even more important than meeting teacher needs. Right now, few teachers or students have those opportunities."

... helping students understand how to pose questions and retrieve information to provide answers — real answers to real questions — is even more important than meeting teacher needs.

"Well, I hear what you are saying, and it sounds convincing, but where's your research? Your opinion — your gut reaction to student and teacher requests — just isn't enough to get me or the MAC to change a schedule that's been in place for years — and that works. Everyone but you seems perfectly happy, Mary. I'm just not sure I want to sign on for the chaos a major change like this will bring."

"I do have research, sir. I have statistics that show how successful both teachers and students think their information search has been when I am available to assist them and when I am not available. I also have been logging teacher and student requests and whether I can fill them, in order to show exactly what can and cannot be accomplished right now. Finally — and this isn't exactly research — I have been doing a few units on the side. I've been working with Donna and Sherry, trying to model as best I could the types of assignments that could be completed if their students had blocks of time in the media center. I think they understand the concept *and* appreciate the difference. Whether or not they appreciate it enough to give up their planning time ... I just don't know."

"Do you have anybody else's research but your own? You certainly haven't sold *me* yet."

"No, sir, not really."

"Well, then, get some. I don't mean to be difficult, Mary, but I've been watching you over the past few months. You're working hard and you're onto something. But you have one opportunity, so you'd better make the best of it. I can't mandate change for an entire school to satisfy only one person, no matter what I personally believe. You'll have to convince the others. You're not there yet."

Mary left the building slowly, replaying the conversation in her mind. Where had she gone wrong? Had she gone wrong? Actually, Mr. Taylor had a good point. She probably should pull together the research on flexible scheduling. After all, she was a librarian! She'd visit the university library Saturday.

Monday morning Mary arrived at school early. She had spent most of the weekend putting the bibliography together and summarizing the research. She'd even given her speech to both her husband and the dog. Photocopying her handouts, she shrugged her shoulders philosophically. No one, not even Mr. Taylor, could accuse her of not being prepared. She had done her best.

That afternoon as everyone straggled in, clutching their drinks and helping themselves to the chocolate candies in the center of the table, Mary began the meeting. Several budget items were dispensed with in short order. Soon she drew a deep breath and began.

"I've been at this school almost three years now, and I really admire what we are able to accomplish. But over the years, I also have been frustrated at what I believe we *could* do if we made one change in the way we approach our schedule. I am proposing that we move the media center schedule to a flexible one, one in which each teacher signs up for time during the school day according to the instructional needs of his or her classroom. I'll be up front with you; this would mean that I would be removed from the planning block. But removing me from the planning block would enable me to plan *with* you to provide more meaningful experiences for your children.

... the school library media field has research that indicates that flexible scheduling in the media center does create an optimum learning environment within the school.

"Before we begin to discuss this, let me distribute some background information. First of all, the school library media field has research that indicates that flexible scheduling in the media center does create an optimum learning environment within the school. The national professional organization, AASL, has a position paper on flexible scheduling which is in your packet of materials.

"But more importantly, many of you have assisted me in pulling together our own research about the need for flexible scheduling. Bob, you and the other fifth-grade teachers have helped your classes complete a survey as they're gathering resources in the media center. This has become the student portion of the curriculum support fill rate you see on the first page of your packet. You all helped me figure the media specialist availability measures you see before you. What I did was log your requests and your students' requests for assistance and categorize them as to whether I could fill those requests. This information is also on the first page of your packet.

"As you can see, everyone is more successful when I am available to help. But the biggest difference comes when I am available to assist students. Notice the difference in their success rates when I am working directly with them. It is significant.

"Now what I'm proposing is radical for this school, so first let me say up front that I would like for us to try flexible scheduling next fall through the holidays. If in January we decide that this is not working, then we'll go back to the old schedule."

"Well, I certainly have seen what can happen when my students have larger blocks of time in the media center," said Donna, "and I've often wished for the opportunity to send several of them to the center on the spur-of-the-moment to get information or quick research. But I can't imagine giving up my planning time, I'm sorry, Mary."

Mary smiled. "I'm not without a possible solution for that dilemma, Donna. Every teacher in kindergarten through the third grade has a full-time assistant. We're already using music, art, and PE as planning times, as well as the media center block. We'll continue to do so. In order to move the media center out of that planning block, however, I propose that we use the K–3 teacher assistants. On the days when each teacher's students have art, music, or PE, they would continue using those times as planning opportunities. Often I will be able to join you as you plan for instruction. But for the times that library time has been used for planning, we would move a primary teaching assistant into a fourth- or fifth-grade classroom only for that planning period. If my calculations are correct, each assistant would have only one upper-grades planning assignment a week — they would leave their own teacher and students only one hour per week."

"It sounds as though you expect those teaching assistants to handle their own classrooms if the planning time falls within library time, is that correct?" Bob asked.

"Exactly."

"I don't mind that, Mary," piped up Rose, a second-grade teacher. "It seems like a small sacrifice, but I am loath to give up my children's weekly story and activity time with you. It is so important that they have this library experience — get in the habit of going to the library, so to speak."

"I couldn't agree more, Rose, and they can still have it — weekly if you want. But it doesn't have to be an hour every week. A story really takes only fifteen or twenty minutes to read and talk about, so with flexible scheduling they can move in and out more often — and they can come in for other things as well. Some of them could even come back that same day — or the next — to learn how to use the encyclopedia or search the Internet. All those things work far better with small groups of students rather than a whole class. And everyone can get that opportunity in one or two days rather than spreading it over a particular week-day for several weeks."

After several more minutes of discussion, Mr. Taylor weighed in. "Frankly, I think Mary may be on to something here. Matter of fact, I checked with several of my colleagues after Mary approached me with this idea last week. Only a few of them have flexible schedules, but those who do are sold on their educational benefits. And I think her proposal is fair. Next fall through January, however, may not give us enough time to get a feel for how this is operating. We'll discuss it in January, but if we vote to implement flexible scheduling, I reserve the right to extend the trial through the school year. There is one price to pay if we decide to do this, however, Mary. You're going to have to help me make the schedule this summer."

Amid chuckles, the MAC cast its vote to try flexible scheduling the next fall. As Mary danced home, she knew that the hard work had just begun. While the MAC had approved the change and Mr. Taylor's support would assure its implementation, flexible scheduling was doomed if she couldn't convince the others of its value. She'd have to use the same data, the same research, and the same enthusiasm to help everyone understand this approach. She had done it once; she could do it again. It was time to celebrate!

Mary's Flexible Schedule Bibliography

American Association of School Librarians and Association for Educational Communications and Technology. *Information Power: Guidelines for School Library Media Programs.* Chicago: American Library Association, 1988.

Barron, D. "Getting Rid of Those Rigid Schedules." *School Library Media Activities Monthly* 5, 2 (October 1988): 49–50.

Browne, Karen Stevens. "Making the Move to Flexible Scheduling — Six Stepping Stones." *School Library Media Activities Monthly* 8, 1 (September 1991): 28–29.

Browne, Karen Stevens, and Linda Burton. "Timing Is Everything: Adapting to the Flexible Schedule." *School Library Journal* 35, 16 (December 1989): 20–23.

Buchanan, Jan. *Flexible Access Library Media Programs.* Englewood, CO: Libraries Unlimited, 1991.

Farwell, Sybil. "Successful Models for Collaborative Planning." *Knowledge Quest* 26, 2 (January/February 1998): 24–30.

Haycock, Carol-Ann. "Cooperative Program Planning: A Model That Works." *Emergency Librarian* 16, 2 (November/December 1988): 29-32.

Hughes, Judy, "Removing the Blocks: Becoming Flexibly Scheduled." *The School Librarian's Workshop* (April 1990): 3–4.

Jay, M. Ellen. "Flexible Scheduling: Potential for Impact." In J.B. Smith (ed.), *School Library Media Annual*, Vol. 7. Englewood, CO: Libraries Unlimited, 1989, pp. 57–60.

Jay, M. Ellen, and Hilda L. Jay. "The Principal and the Library Media Program." *School Library Media Activities Monthly* (April 1990): 30–32.

Lance, Keith. "The Impact of School Library Media Centers on Academic Achievement." *School ibrary Media Quarterly* 22, 3 (Spring 1994): 167–70, 172.

Lankford, Mary D. "Flexible Access: Foundation for Student Achievement." *School Library Journal* 40, 8 (August 1994): 21-23.

Loertscher, David V., May Lien Ho, and Melvin M. Bowie. "Exemplary Elementary Schools and Their Library Media Centers: A Research Report." *School Library Media Quarterly* 15, 3 (Spring 1987): 147-53.

Ohlrich, Karen Browne. "Flexible Scheduling: The Dream vs. Reality." *School Library Journal* 38, 5 (May 1992): 35–38.

Oswald, Marilyn K. "Implementing and Maintaining Successful Flexible Scheduling in Elementary School Library Media Programs." ED375829 (1994).

Putnam, Eleanor. "The Instructional Consultant Role of the Elementary School Library Media Specialist and the Effects of Program Scheduling on Its Practice." *School Library Media Quarterly* 24, 1 (Fall 1996): 43–49.

Shannon, Donna M. "Tracking the Transition to a Flexible Access Library Program in Two Library Power Elementary Schools." *School Library Media Quarterly* 24, 3 (Spring 1996): 155–63.

van Deusen, Jean D. "The Effects of Fixed versus Flexible Scheduling on Curriculum Involvement and Skills Integration in Elementary School Library Media Programs." *School Library Media Quarterly* 21, 3 (Spring 1993): 173–82.

_____. "Prerequisites to Flexible Planning." *Emergency Librarian* 23, 1 (September/October 1995): 16–19.

Weisburg, Hilda, and Ruth Toor. "To Be or Not To Be Flexible: A Philosophical Argument." *The School Librarian's Workshop* (December 1989): 1-2.

Yesner, Bernice L., and Hilda L. Jay. *Operating and Evaluating School Library Media Programs: A Handbook for Administrators and Librarians.* New York: Neal-Schuman, 1998.

Chapter 5

The Case for
a Technology Assistant

Paul looked around his cluttered office. Piles of catalogs and unread journals graced the small table in the center of the room, and books ready for processing were lined up like soldiers on the counters beside the sink — even the small bookcase behind the desk was overflowing with books to be discarded, computer programs waiting to be installed, snags to be searched. And his desk — his desk was a *total* disaster. The only place a teacher, a child, or, worse yet, the principal could leave a note with any assurance that it would be found was in his chair. "Heaven only knows what will happen once the entire building is networked," he despaired.

Too intimidated by the clutter and his vision of the future even to begin his book and software orders due next week, yet too frustrated simply to close the door and go home, he began the daily task of washing up the coffee pot and his lunch dishes in the small sink in the corner of the room. The warm, sudsy water seemed to have a calming effect. For the umpteenth time he searched his brain for the one argument that would convince the administration of the obvious: he needed an assistant. Certainly clutter wouldn't do it. Neither would the simple and best reason: 950 middle school students and 40 teachers who needed his full attention. He feared they never would see him once the network was installed.

As he rinsed the coffee pot, washed out the sink, and filled the pot with water and fresh coffee in readiness for the next day, he stopped short. Wasn't that book he'd ordered — something about school library output measures — over on the counter waiting to be processed?

He'd just begun flipping through the pages when the phone rang. It was Cathy already on her way to pick up the baby at day care. "Don't forget you're going to take Jeremy to soccer this afternoon,

Paul," she reminded him. "I'll start dinner when I get home, but I've got PTA tonight, so we'll have to hurry."

Paul muttered his assent, hung up the phone, and began to pack up. He looked around his office. "I really should take home these journals and work on that software order, however ..." He scooped up the new book. He'd seen just enough to get him interested.

That night after Cathy had left for PTA and he had bathed, read to, and settled the children, Paul dropped into his chair and closed his eyes. Tired as he was, his mind still was swirling. Soon he reached down and pulled the book out of his briefcase. By the time Cathy returned, he had a plan.

The next morning was its usual whirlwind of activity: students returning overnight reference books, teachers grabbing a cup of coffee and a video or software program for their classes, even Mr. Farley the principal checking on the use of the media center for next week's summer honors testing program. Once the students were in homeroom, however, Paul cleared a spot on his desk, poured himself a cup of coffee, and began to sketch out his forms.

... he had decided to use all the measures to justify his need for an assistant ... [but] he realized that, although almost every measure could be used to justify staffing, in reality some were far better than others.

In his enthusiasm the night before, he had decided to use all the measures to justify his need for an assistant. After all, the more evidence he could bring to the table, the stronger would be his case. Yet in the cold light of morning, reason began to take control. There were not enough hours in the day to collect all that information, at least not if he wanted to do his job and continue to justify an assistant. Looking over the correlation matrix in the book, he realized that, although almost every measure could be used to justify staffing, in reality some were far better than others.

Obviously, both the media center use rate and the in-library use needed to be tracked: traffic into the library and the subsequent need for help would be a major factor in his case for an assistant. Likewise, the number of materials used within the center was another compelling piece of information; the circulation rate would certainly be easy to include. He could pull that information off the OPAC at any point.

As he moved down the chart, considering his own program and his relative comfort in using the statistics to justify his case, however, he realized that concentrating on the curriculum support request rate and the troubleshooting request rate was the logical decision. Add to that the media center use rate for verification of activity other than technology, and he should be set. These three measures would give him a strong position from which to justify his need: they would demonstrate the lack of time, now and in the future, to work with students and plan and support teachers. In-library use rate would be nice, but he only had so much time and energy! And even though his messy desk and late paperwork might indicate to him that a clerical assistant would be in order, the political climate in both the school and the school system was encouraging technology. If he were to have any chance at all, he had better concentrate on the best arguments possible for a *technology* assistant. Smiling in satisfaction that a focus had been identified, he got up, put his cup in the sink, and walked out into the center to welcome his first class of the day.

That afternoon in the calm of the deserted media center, Paul worked on the forms that would help him keep track of the library's use. First he created a daily tracking form, making five copies— one for each day the next week. Then he made himself a troubleshooting request form and a curriculum support request form, and photocopied those as well. Rummaging around in the cabinet in the equipment room, he found several clipboards. Once he had everything organized, he turned out the lights and locked the doors. It was time to take Jeremy to yet another soccer game.

Monday morning dawned crisp and beautiful. Paul felt a bit guilty leaving Cathy to get the children to school by herself, but he wanted to make sure everything was in order for his record keeping — and she *had* volunteered. She thought his idea was a good one and she anticipated less take-home work and more evening family time if Paul's project was successful.

The building was almost deserted when he arrived, but the pace soon increased. All of Ms. Wilson's social studies classes moved in and out of the media center, each group looking up its own African nation and using the CD-ROMs, the Internet, and the reference books. Mr. Stevens sent three students to develop a PowerPoint presentation of their science project for the state finals, and what seemed to be every single student in the school needed a new book to read before the daily Drop Everything and Read. Sometime during the middle of all this, the OPAC network went down, the bulb blew on Ms. Sinclair's overhead, and a tape jammed in Ms. Gonzola's machine. When Mr. Farley appeared beside him at lunchtime, Paul knew it was Monday!

"What about coming in to help Ms. Dalton with that new attendance program that the central office wants everyone to use? Say, sometime after you get a quick bite to eat?" As Paul nodded his assent and began to jot down the request on his clipboard, Mr. Farley turned around. "What's that you're doing there? Looks interesting, I guess."

"Well, sir, I'm doing a bit of research here. I'm just keeping track of all the requests that I get from students and teachers to help with the computers and other equipment. It seems to be taking more and more of my time, and I'm beginning to wonder what the impact on my time will be once the network is installed for next year. I thought that perhaps together we might want to put together a proposal for a technology assistant and include it in next year's budget."

"Technology assistant, huh? Logging requests? Sounds like an interesting tactic to me, Paul. I'll look forward to seeing your statistics and justification. It might just work."

Paul smiled to himself as he unwrapped his sandwich and opened a bag of chips. He had set the stage nicely. He just hoped that his data would convince Mr. Farley — and then the school board.

Friday arrived none too soon, and Paul greeted it with mixed emotions. Cathy was taking the children to visit her parents for the weekend. He had opted to stay in town to try to put together his statistics from the week. He wanted Mr. Farley to have ample time to consider his data and suggest changes before school budgets were due at the end of the month. This was a great opportunity for concentrated work, but it certainly would be lonely!

By Sunday afternoon Paul had analyzed his data and written what he believed to be a convincing letter stating his — and the school's — need for a technology assistant. He even had enough time to make his famous spaghetti before Cathy and the children returned. As the flavorful sauce simmered on the stove, he made mental notes to himself for the next day. He'd drop off his letter first thing in the morning and then make an appointment to see Mr. Farley later in the day —hopefully after he'd had a chance to read it. And he'd better tackle that office. While nothing was assured until Mr. Farley and the school board approved the position, he was determined to think positively —and who in the world would want to share that office in its present condition!

Paul's Memo to Mr. Farley

To: Mr. Farley
From: Paul MacGregor
Topic: Justification for a Technology Assistant for
        Barnfield Middle School

Since I joined the faculty in 1992, Barnfield Middle School has grown and expanded. In September 1992, we opened school with 725 students and a faculty of 29; today our student body numbers 950, our faculty 40. In 1992 we had one computer in the media center office for word processing and overdues, one VCR for each grade level, and lots of books. Today we still have lots of books, but we also have 10 VCRs, a jerry-rigged television studio, and a networked media center that comprises an automated catalog and circulation system available on 5 computers, Internet access on 3 computers, and a CD-ROM tower serving 4 computers in the reference area. Plans are also in place to network the entire school this summer. Obviously, the maintenance of equipment and resources has increased substantially over the past 6 years; likewise so have the needs of both students and teachers.

Over the years, I have suspected that more and more of my time has been spent troubleshooting equipment and less of my time has been spent working with teachers and students. In an effort to document this suspicion, I tracked the equipment troubleshooting requests as well as the student and teacher needs for the week of March 3. The information I found was both interesting and compelling.

Page –2–

As you examine the data in charts 1 and 2, please note the following:

- For the purposes of this report, I have used the following definitions:

  — curriculum support request: any request a teacher makes that relates directly to his or her teaching the curriculum.

  — troubleshooting request: any request for assistance in solving an equipment problem. This can range from loading software and instructing in its use, to cleaning VCRs and maintaining the media center network.

- During the week of March 3, I had 67 requests for troubleshooting and 45 requests for curriculum support from the faculty here at Barnfield. I separated these two areas for the sake of this analysis, but in fact they are interrelated. Malfunctioning equipment, whatever the reason, directly impacts instruction. In reality, you can interpret all requests as curriculum support requests.

As you can see from the attached analysis, during the week of March 3, I spent an average of 3.4 hours daily on troubleshooting. Although many of these requests were taken care of before or after school, 67 percent did interrupt my instructional time to some degree. This is in addition to the instructional time lost by the teacher making the request. Of equal concern is the number of curriculum requests made by teachers during that five-day period. I can honestly say that approximately 80 percent of these requests were supported in a way that satisfied the individuals involved, but that means that 20 percent were not. I realize that even in a perfect world 100 percent of the customers will not be satisfied 100 percent of the time, but I am well-aware that the percentage of satisfaction would have been higher if I had been spending less time with equipment issues.

All of the above concern me, yet the statistics that are most troubling are those related to media center use. During the week of March 3, we averaged slightly more than one class a period in the media center. During this same week, each student and teacher in the school averaged approximately two trips to the media center. Although overlapping of visits occurred (students and teachers visiting as *classes* were included in the overall student and teacher totals), this is still very heavy use of the facility and its resources. If 79 percent of the equipment-troubleshooting requests require that I leave the media center, who is assisting these students and teachers while I am gone?

This dilemma will only worsen once the entire building is networked. While some computer-related visits to the media center may decline because equipment and some resources will be accessed from the classroom, the troubleshooting requests are likely to increase. If teachers are to integrate technology into their instruction as the school board has mandated, it must be seamless and transparent. They must be comfortable with the software they are using and secure in the knowledge that the equipment will work when they need it — or that it will be fixed quickly when it does not. This age of myriad resources necessitates learning how to evaluate and use them in the most intelligent and efficient manner. Barnfield needs a media specialist who can concentrate on the curriculum and all the materials and services that support it. As much as I have enjoyed introducing and maintaining a variety of technology to the faculty and students in my role as media specialist, the job has grown beyond one person. In conjunction with the implementation of the network next fall, it is time to bring a technology assistant on board to support the equipment so that I can devote my energies to the teaching and learning here at Barnfield Middle School.

[Figure 5-1]
(Sample Data for Media Center Use for One Week)

Media Center Use Analysis for the Week of March 3

Week of March 3

Total number of equipment troubleshooting requests:	67
Average number of daily requests:	13.4
Total amount of time spent troubleshooting:	970 minutes (16.2 hours)
Average number of hours daily:	3.4
Of the 67 requests, those that involved leaving the media center	53 (79%)
Of the 67 requests, those that involved some interruption in instruction time (my working with students or teachers in any capacity)	45 (67%)

During the same March 3 week:

Number of requests for curriculum support: (average: 1+/teacher during the week)	45
Number of requests completed within time frame considered satisfactory by both media specialist and teacher	36 (80%)
Number of requests completed but modified as to time frame, situation, etc.:	8 (18%)
Number of requests unable to complete:	1 (2%)

[*Figure 5-2*]
(Sample Media Center Use Analysis for One Week)

Page –2–

Media Center Use Analysis for the Week of March 3

Student Body: 950
Teachers: 40

1. Total # of classes visiting media center   35

2. Total # of students (during school day)   1,887
   Total # of students (before/after school)   138

   Total # of student visits   2,025

3. Total # of teachers (during school day)   41
   Total # of teachers (before/after school)   52

   Total # of teacher visits   93

4. Other (parents, administrators, etc.)   16

5. Subjects   16   LA
            10   SS
             5   Career Explorations
             4   Science

6. Grade Level   10   sixth
              15   seventh
              10   eighth

   Highest use day: Tuesday
   Highest use time: 9 – 11 am
   Lowest use day: Friday
   Lowest use time: 2 – 3 pm

Chapter 6

The Case for
Collection Development
before New Course Addition

Block scheduling at Waterside High School had its supporters and detractors. For some students and teachers, it seemed to be ideal, allowing many slower teens more time with a single subject. For the more highly motivated or advanced young person, it offered a chance to take several more courses throughout a high school career, thus giving them an opportunity to explore subjects that they ordinarily would not have been able to fit into their courseload.

But all those extra courses in the schedule were creating havoc with the media center budget. Katrina Lee and Carlos Martinez, the media specialists, constantly were having to scramble, trying to fill holes in their collections as each department brainstormed this new semester's offering. Ms. Justus had always wanted to teach music appreciation; Mr. Bainbridge, Shakespearean tragedy. And the vocational education and family and consumer sciences departments were having a field day: computer repair, business basics, nutrition, infant and child development. Every time the media center staff turned around, a new course was being offered, and inevitably all those students soon were in the media center working on a project or paper. Only at these critical moments were the two librarians finding out whether their collection was capable of supporting that particular curriculum area.

One teacher workday as they both sat surrounded by journals, catalogs, and files, they began discussing a possible system for supporting all the new courses, both from a budgetary standpoint and from an organizational one as well.

"What we really need is a way to predict whether we're going to have the resources that will support these courses," Katrina lamented.

"Surely there's a formula that will help us not only figure out how many books we need but also justify more money to purchase them."

"Well, we do have SACS (Southern Association of Colleges and Schools)," mused Carlos.

"Yes, but that's not specific enough," countered Katrina. "All they say is ten books per student, and they don't say a word about AV or software. If all someone is looking at is numbers, we have no argument, Carlos!"

"That's true," he acknowledged as they both returned to the work at hand.

Suddenly Carlos looked up. "It says here in this review that there's a new book coming out about school media center output measures. This reviewer says there's some sort of chart or something — some way to figure out how many books and things you'll need: potential curriculum support rate. Maybe we ought to get that book and see what it says."

"Fine with me," Katrina agreed. "Let's send that PO through separately so that it will get here more quickly."

A couple of weeks later the book arrived in the morning's mail. It was a busy day, and the two media specialists didn't even have a chance to flip through the pages until late that afternoon. As soon as the last teacher left the center loaded down with books and videos — and several class times scheduled for research — Katrina picked up the book.

"Here it is, Carlos. Potential curriculum support rate. Look at this chart. The author has it broken down into elementary and secondary. Seems she says we'd need 1 book per student in each class, 1 AV, 4 periodicals, and 1 professional resource. I wonder how she came up with that? Hmmm. Seems like this is her chart. Any chance this would work with Ms. Lindgren? Maybe I'll just take this book home and look at it further."

"Well, think about it," Carlos advised. "I'm scheduled to meet with the Curriculum Committee tomorrow. I thought I'd see if we could at least find out what new courses they were contemplating before they're announced in the course packs for the fall. If you think it's got possibilities, we'll take the courses they're most likely to offer and run the numbers. Right now, I'm out of here. I have to pick up Dad's medicine before I go to the gym."

Late the next afternoon Carlos returned from the Curriculum Committee meeting with a smile on his face. "I have them," he announced to Katrina as she finished programming the head-in for the next morning's videotapes. "I feel really successful. I think I've convinced them to take a look at our potential curriculum support rate before they decide which semester they'll schedule which courses. That way, if there is a course that is going to need a collection infusion, we'll have enough time to order the materials and get them on the shelf."

"Good for you!" Katrina said. "I began looking through that book while you were gone, and frankly I'm undecided. It's got a whole lot of measures — media center use rate, curriculum support fill rate, media specialist availability. Perhaps we should use more than just the potential curriculum support rate to make our case."

"Let me see that book," Carlos said. "Show me what you're talking about."

As Katrina scurried around the media center straightening chairs, shelving stray books, and shutting down the computers, Carlos continued to read. When she came back into the office, he looked up. "Well, these all look like measures that we could use at some point, especially the use measures and both of those fill rate ones. But I'm not sure we need anything else but the potential curriculum support rate for this particular job. Seems to me that that's the information we need for the decision at hand. Anything else might just muddy the water."

"That's a good point," Katrina agreed. "And I'm certainly not looking for more work! Let's see if we can't figure out a process tomorrow and get going on this. Guidance is going to want to know about those new courses pretty soon."

The next day was relatively uneventful. Only Mr. Smith's classes cycled through, checking bibliographic information for their research papers. They, and the occasional teacher or group of students, created a quiet hum of activity as Katrina and Carlos began their project.

They had decided to brainstorm and identify the Dewey areas of both the regular and reference collections first, then use the catalog to pull up numbers of titles within each range. Since they eventually would need a precise bibliography of current holdings before placing an order, they agreed that they would create a running list of each appropriate resource as it was identified. That way, they and the various departments would know up front what was available currently for each proposed course and what types of resources would need to be ordered.

Once they began, however, they realized that they weren't comfortable unless they could actually hand examine some of the titles to be sure they were what was needed for that particular course. This meant heading to the shelves, printout and scanner in hand. While this wasn't a perfect plan — some things were checked out — they personally felt that the information they would eventually come up with would reflect the collection more accurately.

The plan was to:

• Identify Dewey areas
• Print out shelf list for those areas
• Go directly to shelves to examine titles and create bibliography.

This took care of the book collection.

They handled the AV much as they had the books, actually using the same printout.

• Use same Dewey areas and printout as books
• Examine titles
• Add AV to the bibliography.

Next were the periodicals. Since the school system just recently had purchased a site license for *ProQuest Platinum* for all the high schools, they were comfortable with their periodical coverage, although both admitted that retrospective magazine coverage could be a potential issue. But Carlos refused even to flag this concern. "Anything that happened before 1990 ought to be reflected adequately in our reference and general collection," he announced confidently. While Katrina was not quite as certain, she agreed that he was probably correct in his assumption.

He dug in his heels on another issue, however. "I guess I'm just old fashioned," he admitted, "but I still want to check our hard-copy holdings of periodicals. I know *ProQuest* updates quickly, but there's just something about knowing that you are going to get this week's *Time* or *Newsweek* ..."

Katrina laughed. "You're exactly right — you are old fashioned, but so am I. I'm sure this woman would say that was unnecessary, but checking hard copies won't take long — and you know the social studies teachers will appreciate that! Let's get on to the other electronic resources."

This particular category was relatively easy, too. They had a networked encyclopedia (and *ProQuest* included *World Book* as well), so the encyclopedia recommendation was in place. And, since they had ten computers in the media center — all with Internet access — they were certain that this was covered as well.

"I know this isn't necessary," Katrina said, "but I would like to take a look at the CD-ROMs that support each course. I sometimes think that students have better luck with CD-ROMs than the Internet, and we did just buy that tower last year." Carlos agreed, so their plan was to:

- Check off encyclopedias and Internet access
- Identify CD-ROMs appropriate for subject specialty
- Add resources to bibliography.

The final area was the professional collection. They both were somewhat chagrined. "We really don't *have* a professional collection," Carlos admitted. "I guess I've always thought that since this was a high-school collection, everything should be shelved together. Do you suppose we should rethink this?"

"Well, I'm not sure we need to change our policy on *where* we have those resources," Katrina responded. "After all, once kids are in high school, some of them are at a pretty sophisticated level, so we may not need to segregate those teacher resources. But it might not hurt to ask the Advisory Committee. Perhaps they'll tell us that a separate area just for teaching materials would be a good idea."

"We can do that at the next meeting," Carlos agreed. "At least we can identify anything in the regular collection that we would target specifically for teachers — no matter where we eventually put it — and get on with this project."

The first course proposal was an easy one for the two librarians — mythology. They printed out a long list of titles, all of which seemed appropriate once they got to the shelves. They easily had 100 percent potential curriculum support rate in the books category. They didn't, however, have any videos or CD-ROMs, so they logged those omissions. "This is great," Katrina enthused. "Perhaps we'll finally get some good use of these 200s! And I guess it won't be very hard to find at least one video for them, although I'm not so sure about a CD-ROM. At least now we know to be on the lookout. This process has potential, Carlos!"

The next course proposal was "The U.S. and the Cold War." This one proved more problematic. First of all, the social studies department anticipated two classes for this offering. This meant that Katrina and Carlos had to figure in twice the number of books necessary to support the proposal. When they did the printout of resources, they also realized that the topics were not as straightforward as those for mythology. Whereas they had single whole books on mythology, they were looking at chapters or portions of books regarding the Cold War.

"I wonder how you handle this," Carlos muttered. "Do we log these as whole books?"

"Well, I look at it this way," Katrina answered. "It seems to me that the rationale is to have enough resources so that each student in a class — or two classes in this case — can have at least one book at a time for a major project. Whether this is simply one good chapter or a whole book on the topic is less important than the fact that there are enough materials to go around. That's the issue here, don't you think?"

"That sounds reasonable," Carlos agreed. "At least we have a place to start planning. Let's keep going."

Pretty soon another decision needed to be made. Would they simply declare the book category as 0 percent fill rate, or would they delineate the actual percentage?

"Frankly," said Katrina,"I don't want anyone thinking we don't have *any* books on the Cold War! I vote for figuring the actual percentage." Since Carlos felt equally strongly that the count should reflect the reality of the collection, they agreed to figure the actual percentage fill rate.

The next week Carlos returned to the Curriculum Committee with the potential curriculum support rate report. When he had finished his presentation, Ms. Lindgren the principal spoke up. "We really appreciate your and Katrina's hard work, Carlos. You've given us some important information to consider before we introduce our new courses. I guess I have only one question, however. I notice here that you have a rubric, so to speak, of the numbers of books and things that you should have — a baseline to compare our collection with an ideal one. Where did you get those numbers?"

"That rubric is from a book we used that outlined this process," Carlos explained. "You'll notice the citation at the bottom of the report."

"Yes, I see that, Carlos. But where did the author get *her* data?"

"Frankly, I believe that this is her chart. She says in the book that the numbers are arbitrary — 'benchmarks for comparison' is her term, I believe. They are, however, based on her work with schools and collections over a fifteen-year period, and both Katrina and I feel her benchmarks are certainly valid, if not a bit conservative."

"Well, I must admit that I'm impressed with your analysis. You have certainly forced us to think about our time frame for adding courses to the curriculum. Whether intentionally or unintentionally, you and Katrina have guided us in the direction of better decision making both for next year's courses and for all course additions in the future. Thank you."

" … you have a rubric, so to speak, of the numbers of books and things that you should have — a baseline to compare our collection with an ideal one. Where did you get those numbers?"

Carlos' and Katrina's Report to the Curriculum Committee

Potential Curriculum Support Rate for Proposed Courses:
Waterside High School Media Center Report

Submitted by Katrina Lee and Carlos Martinez

At the March 27 meeting of the Waterside High School Curriculum Committee, the following new courses were proposed for Fall 1999:
- Greek and Roman Mythology (English Department)
- The U.S. and the Cold War (Social Studies Department)
- Marriage and the Family (Family and Consumer Science)

In order to evaluate how the media center resources will support the research, teaching, and individual student-interest needs of these courses, the media specialists analyzed the collection and now present the following information.

[Figure 6-1]

Sample Potential Curriculum Support Rate for Unit on Greek and Roman Mythology

Potential Curriculum Support Rate

Date: 4/2/99

Topic: Greek and Roman Mythology

Department: English

Date to be implemented: 8/11/99

Resource	Adequate	Actual	Percentage/Actual	
Books (ref/fic/non)	1/student/class	44	20%	20%
AV	1	0	20%	0%
Periodicals (includes full-text databases)	4	4 +	20%	20%
Electronic resources (not CD-ROM periodicals)	1 encyclopedia; 1 subject-related and/or 1 Internet sta./class	2 10 Internet sta.	20%	20%
Professional	1	3	20%	20%
			100%	80%

[Figure 6-2]

Sample Potential Curriculum Support Rate for
Unit on the U.S. and the Cold War

Potential Curriculum Support Rate

Date: 4/4/99

Topic: The U.S. and the Cold War

Department: Social Studies

Date to be implemented: 8/11/99

Resource	Adequate	Actual	Percentage/Actual	
Books (ref/fic/non)	1/student/class*	35	20%	14%
AV	1	0	20%	0%
Periodicals (includes full-text databases)	4	4+ (ProQuest)	20%	20%
Electronic resources (not CD-ROM periodicals)	1 encyclopedia; 1 subject-related and/or 1 Internet sta./class	2 10 Internet sta.	20%	20%
Professional	1	0	20%	0%
			100%	54%

*Two classes proposed, so book needs double.

[Figure 6-3]

Sample Potential Curriculum Support Rate for Unit on Marriage and the Family

Potential Curriculum Support Rate

Date: 4/8/99

Topic: Marriage and the Family

Department: Family/Consumer Science

Date to be implemented: 8/11/99

Resource	Adequate	Actual	Percentage/Actual	
Books (ref/fic/non)	1/student/class	27	20%	20%
AV	1	3	20%	20%
Periodicals (includes full-text databases)	4	4+ (ProQuest)	20%	20%
Electronic resources (not CD-ROM periodicals)	1 encyclopedia; 1 subject-related and/or 1 Internet sta./class	2 10 Internet sta.	20%	20%
Professional	1	3	20%	20%
			100%	100%

Source: Charts taken from *Output Measures for School Library Media Centers* by Frances Bryant Bradburn (New York: Neal Schuman, 1999).

Analysis of Data

- Waterside Media Center can support the research, teaching, and reading interests of students and teachers for the "Marriage and Family" course without a major infusion of materials.

- Waterside Media Center also can support the research, teaching, and reading interests of students and teachers for the "Greek and Roman Mythology" course; however, students and teachers will be better served if AV and CD-ROM needs can be filled before the beginning of fall semester.

- Waterside Media Center needs a major collection development initiative before "The U.S. and the Cold War" course is offered, especially since two classes are proposed. The book collection is inadequate to support student research needs, and the AV and professional resources also need to be addressed. The Internet will meet some research needs, but it cannot support the retrospective information requirements — primary documents, historical perspective — currently offered by print resources.

Recommendations

- Waterside Media Center can support the introduction of both the "Marriage and Family" and the "Greek and Roman Mythology" courses for Fall 1999.

- We recommend that the social studies department wait until the spring 2000 semester to offer "The U.S. and the Cold War" courses in order that we have both time and adequate budget to order and process a variety of resources that will enhance this particular course content.